Globalizing Concern for
Women's Human Rights

Globalizing Concern
for Women's Human Rights
The Failure of the American Model

Diana G. Zoelle

St. Martin's Press
New York

149894

ISBN 0–312–22285–8

Library of Congress Cataloging-in-Publication Data
Zoelle, Diana.
    Globalizing concern for women's human rights / by Diana Zoelle.
        p.   cm.
    Includes bibliographical references and index.
    ISBN 0-312-22285-8 (cloth)
    1. Women's rights—Government policy—United States.   2. Human rights—
Government policy—United States.   3. Women's rights—International coopera-
tion.   4. Human rights—International cooperation.   5. United Nations.
Committee on the Elimination of Discrimination Against Women   I. Title.
HQ1236.5.U6 Z64   2000
323.3'4—dc21   99–055570
                                                                                         CIP

Design by Letra Libre, Inc.

First Published: July, 2000
10   9   8   7   6   5   4   3   2   1

In memory of my beloved uncle,
James Wiley Spurk

Contents

Acknowledgments

Like most authors, I have incurred much debt in the course of my work on this manuscript.

Probably no long-term effort is ever completed absent significant influences, particularly of those people close to us. As I recall people who have influenced my thinking, I am reminded that this experience has given me more than it could ever have cost me in time and energy. Throughout my struggle to formulate, complete, and finally revisit this manuscript, many wonderful people taught me about the joy to be found in intellectual, emotional, and psychological connection. Some of them must be mentioned here.

The people who directly influenced the early stages of my writing are relatively easy to identify and, of course, impossible to thank adequately. The faculty and staff in the Department of Government and Politics at the University of Maryland-College Park are all ineradicably etched in my memory. Richard Claude was the single most important influence in my choice of topic. He challenged me to take my interest in feminist theory beyond the narrow boundaries I had set for myself. Ron Terchek's unfailing support while I explored my topic and his confidence in me provided a solid foundation for my work. Jim Glass and Richard Brown provided invaluable critiques of early drafts of the manuscript. Virginia Haufler and Melissa Matthes patiently and meticulously assessed the clarity and structural and theoretical soundness of the entire manuscript. While they may not agree entirely with some of my assertions, all these people have informed my thinking and, in some sense, directed the course of my career.

I owe immeasurable gratitude to the faculty and staff of the Joan B. Kroc Institute for International Peace Studies at Notre Dame for providing an atmosphere conducive to the substantive development of my research. Patricia Davis, RaimoVayrynen, and George Lopez made my two years at the institute as a visiting scholar possible. During my stay at Notre Dame, the Department of Government and International Studies provided me the opportunity to teach a course investigating the topic of women's rights as human rights. Developing the course and discussing ideas with my students aided significantly in furthering my research.

Yet, it is the friends who have enriched my life and the wonderful memories we share and continue to create that confound my efforts to limit my love and gratitude to a manageable number of words and pages. Cindy Burack afforded me the safety to explore and to trust my own insights and ideas ("trusting my own ideas" involved actually submitting the manuscript for publication). Stacy Vandeveer read, critiqued, and encouraged me to rework chapter 4 and, while all the errors are still mine, his insight and clarity were invaluable. Laree Martin taught me a lot about straightforwardness and simplicity. Jyl Josephson has provided for me an unfailing model of industry and integrity. Alayna Waldrum continually challenges my recurring assumption that life, particularly mine, is a serious matter. Jean Downing's generosity, in both time and emotional support, renews my faith in the fundamental goodness of human beings, and Scott Wein made technological "magic" happen at a time when I was in despair.

Finally, I must thank my two wonderful sons, Tom and Chris, who continue to love the unorthodox woman who emerged rather late in her tenure as their mother.

Preface

In 1991, I was discussing women's human rights with Richard Claude at the University of Maryland-College Park. My interest was the ill-defined status of women within international human rights discourse. Initially, I believed that western feminist theory could provide a basis for women's claims. Yet, my attempts to integrate the two areas were fraught with obstructions. The lack of communication between feminist organizations in the United States and activists in international human rights organizations concerned with violations of women's human rights proved to be a very real limitation in my early investigation of the topic. If no one was interested, maybe there was nothing of interest. Maybe the issue was a dead end. Nonetheless, I continued my search. Looking back, I realize that the relative absence of theorizing about women's rights on an international scale, especially by theorists in the United States, offered me the opportunity to investigate an exciting and important area of human rights theory.

Human rights theory was a new area of interest for me and it seemed that I was struggling to connect two bodies of knowledge—western feminist theory and women's international human rights—that were ineluctably separate. Thus, my attempts to make the argument that the International Convention on Elimination of All Forms of Discrimination Against Women (CEDAW) could be a vehicle for achieving gender equity in the United States—in light of the failure of the Equal Rights Amendment—were similarly disheartening. None of the approximately 15 national women's organizations that I contacted in Washington, D.C., was able to provide the information I needed about the status of CEDAW in the United States, which could only mean that they were not interested, that there was no basis for my assumption. Only after considerable effort did I come to realize that domestic organizations and international organizations in the United States were—on this issue, at least—entirely separate. In hindsight, I realize that it should not have surprised me that virtually no communication seemed to be occurring between domestic women's organizations and international women's organizations. Feminist theory within the United States was decidedly "domestic." Even had the women's organizations been interested in

CEDAW, the likelihood of its ratification by the United States was so remote that it would be foolish to pursue CEDAW as an alternative. The emerging "theories of difference" that have been applied to women within U.S. contentions and contexts, can be applied as well to international questions. But, one "does" either domestic *or* international women's rights.

International human rights theory, though, also segregated women's human rights from the broader scope of its debate. In fact, human rights theorists and activists seemed to be struggling to establish concern for human rights as a fundamental, even legitimate, issue within international relations, so it seemed presumptuous to bother them with what they considered a "peripheral" issue. For example, in 1993 I had an exchange with a noted human rights theorist. In the course of our discussion, I raised the question of women's rights. To my chagrin, he replied: "Diana, we're talking about human rights, not women's movements." So, although human rights was becoming a legitimate concern in international affairs and gendered critiques of traditional international relations conceptions were slowly emerging, none of the mainstream theories seemed to launch its critique from the perspective of violations of women's human rights. Consequently, in so far as human rights remained on the fringes of the study of politics and international relations, violations of women's rights were relegated to a much more distant periphery. Yet, there was another aspect of my dis-ease.

As I began to speak about human rights in academic settings in the United States, I realized that, almost inevitably, the discussion turned immediately to condemnation of the violations of human rights *in other countries*. The discussion never moved naturally to questions about U.S. responsibility or the importance of ratification of human rights documents in the United States. Finally, my concerns—primarily with regard to U.S. exemption from culpability, and tangentially connected to my concern about the profound disconnect between international and domestic theories about women—crystallized: The pervasive assumption was that human rights violations did not happen in the United States. The "lines of defensiveness" seemed to go something like this: First, they (those other countries) are inherently different. Second, if isolated and infrequent violations did occur in the United States, they were of no real consequence, but were rather oversights or mistakes. Finally (when backed to the wall), relative to other states, the United States was the undeniable leader in this area and would in fact rectify its own shortcomings.

At this juncture, and with some doubts about the strength of my argument, I accepted the offer to teach a course on women's human rights in the Department of Government and International Studies at the University of Notre Dame. The course was an investigation as to whether the U.S. sociopolitical, legal, and economic systems could be implicated in the continued lack of attention to human rights violations, both in the United States and elsewhere. Surely we would not find that the United States, in fact, perpetuated violations through its policies? I tried to impress upon my students that the violation of human rights is not a relative thing, that is, lesser violations are not absolved by virtue of the existence of greater violations. My further assertion was that we (all nations) have a common responsibility that requires involvement in the process of ratification. So, I charged my students with responding to certain questions. First, in (selectively) allowing other considerations to take precedence over human rights in its foreign policy decisions, is the United States abetting violating states in their abusive behavior? Second, is U.S. refusal to submit itself to scrutiny through ratification, in effect, an a priori absolution of itself? I came away from that course convinced that until feminist (and other) scholars and policymakers in the United States recognize and give voice to the lessons that might be learned from other cultures, human rights violations will remain an issue related only to "those others."

This book is a beginning for me. My work has led me to the understanding that the United Nations has a mixed press. Many believe that the UN *is* its history: a powerless instrument of imperialist goals; a meaningless body, lacking in real focus; an ineffective, ungainly instrument of peace. The United Nations is, in my view, all and none of these things. These views of the United Nations have been its burden and, at the same time, are the reason that it still exists. No other form of organization could have survived as well within such a contentious international milieu. Had the UN been set up to assert itself in any way that could have been perceived as aggressive while it was still in its infancy, it would have self-destructed. Had it spent the last several decades, not developing instruments of peace and processes of diplomatic negotiation, but acting without a strong foundation it would have disintegrated. The UN has been used, misused, and abused, but it still exists and we should be thankful. Those decades spent developing instruments, regimes, and regional bodies should, in hindsight, be recognized as the fortunate—however quixotic—preparation for orderly structuring of global relationships that are mindful of difference and respectful of other.

Introduction 🕊

I n recent years, the international community has given considerable attention to the socioeconomic development of various countries around the globe and the effects of the changing conditions on women's lives. Awareness of women's human rights within the process of development was initiated and has been sustained almost exclusively by nongovernmental organizations.[1] The reports of these organizations have been increasingly encouraging in the last two decades. However, if consideration of women's human rights is to be an integral part of development planning, a sea change must occur in which women are seen as developers rather than simply one of the subjects or, what is more problematic, simply usable tools of development.[2]

The United States continues to be in the forefront of development efforts, both practically and theoretically. Yet, there is a curious absence of theorizing in the United States about this country's role in the promotion of international concern for women's human rights. Popular opinion in the United States is that "the problem" of human rights abuse exists primarily, if not exclusively, outside the United States and falls therefore under the purview of foreign affairs—an area that is rarely central to public debate in America. Human rights as a category of investigation and an arena for social activism has been consigned to international relations theorists and international human rights organizations respectively. Even women's rights organizations in the United States focus solely on domestic issues. International human rights organizations, only lately concerned with women's rights, have focused on monitoring and reporting on abuses outside the United States.[3] The lack of strong connection and meaningful communication between domestic and international organizations about the role of the United States in modeling and supporting concern for women's human rights is key to continued U.S. resistance to ratification of particular human rights documents. If more people outside the human rights community in the United States could be persuaded that strengthening ties with the United Nations was necessary to the stabilization of international relationships, now as well as in the future, key senators in the United States Congress would find it more difficult to block ratification of important treaties.[4]

The International Convention on the Elimination of All Forms of Discrimination against Women (CEDAW) is the first international treaty to provide comprehensive protection of women's human rights. To some degree, the U.S. refusal to ratify CEDAW is similar at its base to U.S. resistance to other major treaties. Yet, resistance to CEDAW is further founded upon continuing legal, political, and societal views as to the appropriate role of women, the structure of the traditional nuclear family, and the economic interests of the state.

Because the United States is a liberal, democratic state founded upon ideals of freedom and equality, its failure to ratify major international human rights treaties appears to be an anomaly. It is not. The central argument of this text is that liberal democracy, as it was conceived and has developed in the United States, is a problematic model in globalizing concern for women's human rights. The position I take is that the U.S. model is progressive and ameliorative *relative* to many others, but that is not good enough; not as good as is possible for a country like the United States.[5] The further argument is that non-ratification of CEDAW is not surprising given U.S. behavior with regard to other human rights treaties. My recommendation is that the United States, through ratification of the International Covenant on Economic, Social, and Cultural Rights (ICESCR) and CEDAW, revisit its fundamental premises and rediscover, within a more enlightened period, the meaning of its commitment to human rights.

This study is not a comparative examination of state exclusion and oppression of women. Neither is it an attempt to distinguish the United States in the larger sense from other Western liberal democratic regimes in its treatment of women. Rather, this study is a gender-sensitive examination of specific dynamics and characteristics inherent to the sociopolitical, economic, and legal systems of the United States that have precluded incorporation of the rights of women on an equal basis with the rights of men. The interaction of these dynamics and characteristics describes a uniquely American national and historical view that serves to render the United States a troublesome exemplar for state incorporation of the human rights of women. Unreserved ratification of CEDAW constitutes a strong indication of effort, by the ratifying state, to protect the human rights of women. The United States has not ratified CEDAW. These facts suggest a need for critique of the institutional structures and cultural dynamics that pose obstructions to ratification.

The obstructions to ratification of CEDAW in the United States are several: First, the U.S. failure to ratify major human rights treaties is a manifestation of the attitudes of elitism and isolationism that continue to prevail in the foreign relations of United States.[6] Second, there is a deep structural resistance in the United States to interference in or modification of what is alleged to be essentially and irrevocably private. Admittedly, the nature of privacy has changed as the increasing presence of women in the public arena has raised questions about what constitutes a public issue. Still, while the parameters of the public arena have altered to accommodate women's presence, definitions and perceptions of agency continue to require women to take on the characteristics of the traditionally recognized male agent.[7] These perceptions have obscured distinctions among the various races, classes, and ethnicities of women under the rubric of the ostensibly more important commonalities—distinctions that have not been addressed sufficiently in public forums. Also, strong sociopolitical rhetoric and cultural pressures are implicated in women's continued marginalization. The dominant rhetoric concerning women's physical absence from the "home" evokes a kind of vacuum that threatens to draw them inexorably back to their "natural" place. Thus, culturally ingrained behaviors and systemically embedded institutions continue to locate women primarily in the private realm and only tangentially, through exceptional effort or special circumstances, in the public arena. All of this despite the significant changes women have made in the conditions of their own lives and the growing awareness of the ways that such rhetoric neither describes the world in which we live nor the women who help to people it.

A third obstruction is that the pluralist nature of American society serves to strengthen an unyielding grip on individualist conceptions of rights and privileges. The negative rights and clearly circumscribed privileges that have centered around a male standard have, thus, become problematic in attempting to understand women's reality. Increasingly, questions of privacy have centered, for women, on the body. The definitions of rights that emerge from this discourse require more of the state and are significantly more complex than the privacy provided in the Lockean civil society. The challenge presented by these questions of privacy is to determine whether it is possible to address women's rights within such narrowly circumscribed conceptions of individuality given, for example, women's reproductive capacity.

The fourth obstruction is that Americans' view of themselves as struggling to maintain what is "private" against the state has to do with a particular form of individualism—a view that encompasses psychological, economic, and moral and theological dimensions. This creates a dilemma for women. Their protections against state intervention are counterpoised with the need for positive action by the state to ensure institutionalization of practices and the availability of services that provide for situations and needs that are peculiar to women.

It would be prudent of the United States to engage in the incorporation and further development of the international human rights instruments that establish the terms of global cooperation and peaceful development. Yet, the

United States resists ratification and incorporation of the very international human rights treaties it helped to devise. Global conditions of restructuring also offer a unique opportunity for the United States to position itself, once again, as a world leader.[8] Yet the United States remains unwilling to engage in self-reflexive criticism of its own shortcomings and to open itself to foreign scrutiny.

As the new millennium approaches, the world is moving inexorably toward increasing global cooperation and interdependency. The reduction in bipolar tension and the process of restructuring in the international system and various states offer unique opportunities for positive change. The potential exists to accord human rights to all people in a world community that is less torn apart by bipolar enmity, less subverted by ideological tensions, and less compromised by the economic priorities of multinational corporations. In according human rights issues the prominence they deserve, states are in truth realizing a new ordering of priorities on two counts—each within its own cultural, economic and political context and in relationship to the world community. These factors constitute a compelling argument for greater involvement by the United States, both to fulfill its obligation as a world citizen and to reclaim the theoretical base of its own system through incorporation of human rights standards.

In order to situate the specific argument that the United States provides a problematic model in globalizing concern for women's human rights within a context, chapter 1 distinguishes between civil and human rights in state fulfillment of the claims of liberalism. The chapter makes the argument that the United States must evaluate its behavior toward its citizens not in comparison with other ostensibly lesser regimes, rather it must determine its level of consistency with its own rhetoric concerning the fundamental principles and premises of its own system. The chapter conveys the basis of the conflict that underlies much of the disenfranchisement that occurs in U.S. political, legal and socioeconomic systems by outlining the tension between the U.S. view of itself as the embodiment of human rights values and its practical limitations—particularly in terms of its identification of *conferred* civil rights as commensurate with and sufficient to the purpose of *inherent* human rights.

Chapter 1 ultimately questions (1) the adequacy of U.S. law to address violations of women's human rights within its own system, and (2) the capacity of the United States (as a world leader) to argue that its behavior serves as an example of commitment to human rights. The initial sections deny the capacity of civil rights legislation to remedy human rights violations—either perceptually or practically—and question whether the United States can legitimately exempt itself from ratification of international human rights instruments. Also, this first chapter provides the groundwork for the argument that major international instruments—though they constitute significant strides toward global communication and cooperation—suffer under, and essentially reify, state failure to regard women.

Chapter 2 focuses on CEDAW. It provides a working knowledge of the treaty and illustrates the ways that CEDAW extends beyond civil and political rights for women by incorporating the demand that states acknowledge responsibility for cultural, social, and economic conditions that directly affect women. As the only international human rights instrument that focuses specifically and comprehensively on women's human rights, CEDAW provides a necessary augmentation to the major international human rights instruments. The major treaties, the International Covenant on Civil and Political Rights (ICCPR) and the International Covenant on Economic, Social, and Cultural Rights (ICESCR), fail to penetrate substantially the boundaries of the private realm in which women are located in virtually all societies and thus fall short of protection of women's rights. CEDAW does penetrate those boundaries. It carefully outlines both general and specific remedies for the systemic inequities and oppressive societal biases that have limited women's participation and equal operation within state systems. It forces an interrogation of traditional norms and standards and requires each state party to assume an active role in eliminating and/or mitigating the gender-based inequitable treatment of its citizens.

In light of the failure of ICCPR and ICESCR to provide the protections necessary to alleviate harms to women—as women, this chapter proposes CEDAW as the instrument that augments their provisions in order to extend human rights protections to women. Accordingly, the first six articles of CEDAW are set forth and examined in turn. The primary purpose of this examination is to delineate clearly the nature of women's harms. The secondary purpose is to indicate the responsibility of the state to engage actively in the process of eliminating those harms. In other words, rather than remaining bound by a priori considerations of the negative rights of "full citizens," states must be willing to take positive action to alter conditions that govern women's exclusion. The U.S. system serves as the "test case" in examining the pervasive, transhistoric exclusion of women primarily because it is the least suspect in terms of failure to address women's rights and frankly because it would benefit by critical self-analysis.

Chapter 3 is an overview of the complexities of international and state resistance to globalizing concern for women's human rights. This chapter advances the argument that protection of the human rights of women is an international as well as a domestic issue, and that the U.S. effort to protect women could be informed by the international struggle. The effort to embrace commonality and difference within the international struggle for women's human rights significantly altered the women's movement in the mid-1970s in the United States. The narrow feminist discourse that had worked against cooperative efforts among women of differing races, classes, and orientations within the United States became painfully obvious under the scrutiny and criticism of non-Western women in 1975 during the first International Women's Conference in Mexico City. The chapter further illustrates the systemic, legal, and member-state normative obstructions to women's human rights within the UN itself and makes the claim that these obstructions represent an international reinscription of the traditional, patriarchal structures of member states. It is, therefore, primarily a gendered analysis of UN bodies and structures and secondarily, an introduction to the idiosyncrasies of state relationships within the UN system. Before turning, in the following chapter, to the particular dynamics and characteristics of the United States, the chapter establishes a context for the debate over women's international human rights by discussing the international environment within which the debate occurs. Chapter 3 is ultimately a critique of the lack of gender representation in UN bodies, the patriarchal biases of those bodies and the function of Western liberal democratic ideology in the formation of those biases. The analysis focuses indirectly on CEDAW, using it as the exemplar of U.S. noninvolvement in human rights treaty ratification.

Chapter 4 examines U.S. ambivalence regarding ratification of international human rights treaties in general and suggests several reasons for U.S. failure to accord due prominence to human rights in its foreign policy. The chapter provides a historical analysis of the context in which women's human rights gained international attention and the less than stellar role of the United States in that struggle. It outlines two dynamics that have been central to U.S. unwillingness to commit to a coherent policy on human rights in its foreign affairs: first, the priorities of the Cold War years; and, second, abiding attitudes of elitism and (a peculiar form of) isolationism in the United States. I argue that these dynamics have presented critical and persistent obstructions to universal recognition of the importance of human rights protections. Further, it is primarily through the efforts of grassroots and nongovernmental organizations (NGOs) that human rights protection has remained a viable issue.

Ultimately, I draw a parallel between the challenge to traditional international law represented by international human rights law and the challenge to traditional domestic law represented by state recognition of women's rights. This parallel in national and international structures is simply an interesting notion until one recognizes the hierarchical nature of the two systems. In effect, women are "twice removed" from major international human rights protections. However, I argue that universal ratification of CEDAW could (1) establish an international dialogue in which women's rights are present, (2) enhance the process wherein NGO implementation occurs, and (3) encourage renewed focus by international financial institutions and corporations on women as participants in development rather than simply resources to be utilized for predetermined ends.

Finally, chapter 5 argues that as a world leader, the United States, by refusing to ratify CEDAW, undermines the effective incorporation of both domestic and international human rights protections for women and limits its effectiveness as a world leader in the area of human rights. Chapters 4 and 5 set out the fundamental problems that surround negotiation and ratification of human rights treaties in general within international fora, but ultimately investigate the various bases of resistance to discussion of women's human rights within United Nations mainstream bodies based upon the traditional patriarchal structures of member states themselves. Chapter 5 brings together the arguments of previous chapters focusing on particular limitations for women within the liberal democratic system as it has developed in the United States. It highlights the need to incorporate "difference" in the normative construction of any political discourse, yet moves beyond the feminist liberal legal argument that posits difference as in direct tension with equality. It offers what amounts to a rethinking of traditional ideas of individualism and autonomy in the United States. In an effort to transcend the contemporary debate around women's rights that posits equality and difference as diametrically opposed, the chapter proposes, in Zillah Eisenstein's terms, a "radicalization" of liberal democracy, using Robin West's argument for acts of power in public as well as private life that are loving and Evelyn Fox Keller's conception "dynamic autonomy."

This final chapter also restates the claim that civil rights legislation in the United States is inadequate in its capacity to provide a remedy for U.S. failure to honor the human rights of more than half of its citizens. In effect, civil rights in the United States have constituted a "civil facade" which in the late twentieth century is rapidly disintegrating. Thus, the time has passed for isolated remedial action within each state. Any effective remedy to the oppression and exclusion of women is, at this point in history, ultimately an international one. A remedy that reaches into the private realm in which women are found globally and within which their harms are contained. Women have gained so much ground in global efforts to identify their common oppression that returning to state-limited remedies would constitute a denial of the power of their unity and of their obligations to one another— the recognition of which has only emerged through several decades of dialogue. Much would be lost in energy and authority if women could not rely for legitimation upon the efforts of the past three decades and the instrument that resulted from those efforts. The fundamental assumption of this work is that universal ratification of CEDAW is a propitious avenue for expanding the dialogue and for reclaiming the virtues of fundamental human rights for all citizens of the world.

Chapter 1 🐦

"Ain't I a Human?"

U.S. Civil Rights Legislation as an Inadequate Remedy to Violations of Women's Human Rights

> The investigation of the rights of the slave has led me to a better understanding of my own. I have found the Anti-Slavery cause to be the high school of morals in our land—the school in which *human rights* are more fully investigated, and better understood and taught, than in any other.[1]
>
> —Angelina Grimke, 1991

Women's international struggle to overcome their differences and find a coherent public voice in defense of their human rights constitutes a significant victory over cultural biases and demographic particularities.[2] The relative success of their efforts has required unyielding respect for—even, finally, reliance upon—each other's differences. Women found that they could maintain the seemingly untenable balance between cooperation in service of their various objectives and co-optation by what could easily have become another exclusionary and monolithic discourse representing only those who commanded the resources to impose their wills. From this nebulous space of hard-won, though tentative, consensus, women have attempted to express their concerns within their own cultural contexts.[3]

The responses to women's efforts within their own states have been various. Since the focus of this study is the response of the United States, this chapter examines the inadequacy of civil remedies within the liberal democratic system in the United States to redress what amount to human rights violations against women. The remedial inadequacy of civil legislation would be less egregious if the United States were willing to include discussion of international standards in its public discourse and engage in serious debate as to the efficacy of those standards in addressing what appear to be ineradicable problems within its own system. But, even as it neglects the examination of its own shortcomings, the United States invariably chooses to "police" the behavior of states that have ratified international treaties.[4] Within the United States, this responsibility has been viewed as the burden of being the superpower. However, the complexities of U.S. international relationships and U.S. ordering of domestic priorities require a more thorough analysis. The salient issues are these: (1) the most enduring domestic problems that the United States faces are gender and race relations in this country; (2) unless these problems are made a matter of widespread public concern and meaningful debate in light of the growing importance of international consensus, the United States will remain profoundly conflicted in its approach to its social problems and complacent with regard to its global responsibilities; and (3) if the United States remains unreflexively complacent with regard to its commitments, this will inevitably lead to increased diffidence in international relationships. Committing itself to ratification of human rights treaties and, thus, subjecting its own system to analysis constitutes an effort to address both domestic problems and global responsibilities. The first and most critical concern is addressing the lingering, though politically displaced, definition of "humanness" in the United States.

The History of "Humanness" in the United States

The United States is a liberal democracy, born of revolution in protest of nonrepresentative rule. The Declaration of Independence of the United States calls for "freedom and equality for all." Yet, that declaration was signed by slave-holding, white male landowners. Eighty years after the signing of the declaration, at the height of the Civil War, the Gettysburg Address represented a "new founding" of the ideals iterated in the declaration, and the Emancipation Proclamation constituted the essence of that renaissance. Again, despite these powerful assertions of freedom and equality, approximately one hundred years after the emancipation of slaves, Martin Luther King Jr. and Malcolm X found it necessary to struggle for the civil rights that they thought might give substantive meaning to that emancipation.[5] Thirty years after the assassinations of Martin Luther King Jr. and Malcolm X—and fully 210 years after the signing of the Declaration of Independence—U.S. Supreme Court Justice Sandra Day O'Connor, in *Richmond* v. *Croson Com-*

pany (1989), rendered an opinion concerning minority hiring and subcontracting. In that opinion, she declared that "we are a color-blind society."[6] Ignoring, for a time, the irony of that declaration, we turn to the question of women.

As the epigraph implies, white women in their early struggles for equality, drew upon the similarities between the status of women and the status of African Americans in the history of the United States. Denial of full citizenship and the resulting invisibilization of each group as human beings have continued to be issues of critical importance in this country. Hence, they must be taken out, shaken off, and held up for inspection periodically. The factors that served to invisibilize women and African Americans in this country are several. First, the original absence of constitutional protection was evident in that the counting of "persons" for census or to justify the relative number of representatives for a given voting district. A male slave was counted as three-fifths of a person and women were not counted at all. Martha Nussbaum makes a particularly persuasive argument for the use of the term "human being" rather than "person."[7] In her essay, she cites examples of both the U.S. Supreme Court and lower courts denying certain rights based on the question whether the category "person" was limited to males. She claims:

> With "person" the defender of equality is on uncertain ground, ground that the opponent can at any moment shift under her feet. With "human being," on the other hand, it is always open to her to say to the opponent, "Look at these beings: you cannot fail to grant that they use their senses, that they think about the future, that they engage in ethical conversation, that they have needs and vulnerabilities similar to your own. Grant this, and you grant that they are human. Grant that they are human and you grant that they have needs for flourishing that exert a moral pull on anyone who would deny them."[8]

Second, women and slaves were not recognized as contributing to production. Because slaves had neither autonomy nor agency, their labor could not be considered in the any way theirs and, thus, could not warrant compensation. The value of their labor accrued to their master who, unlike themselves, had control over the means of production (that is, land and slaves) and existed and had agency within the system. Women's labor, both productive and reproductive, was private and therefore neither compensated nor valuated. The fruit of women's labor also accrued to the master or representative male: White women's male children were legitimate heirs to their father's property and slave women's children were property of the master to be sold or otherwise used. Finally, in the writing of history, the conditions of women's and slaves' lives were coherent only in relation to legitimate, full citizens (that is, white, propertied males) and through the lens of that relationship. Slaves were the capital property and means of production and reproduction of capital for slaveowners. White women were the chattel of landowners and the means of reproduction of heirs. Neither had an autonomous public existence. Neither was afforded full citizenship.

These conditions were somewhat altered when amendments were introduced to the Constitution that prohibited state action against African Americans on the basis of race. Later, citizenship rights and the right to vote were conferred by constitutional amendment. Women were granted the right to vote by constitutional amendment also, though not until well after African American men. All other citizenship rights for women were acquired through case law only. Civil rights legislation, in particular Title VII, was originally meant to confer equal citizenship rights on African Americans. "Sex," as a protected category, was added to Title VII as an "afterthought."[9] In all ways women have enjoyed less emphasis on their status as citizens, primarily because women are considered, according to most early liberal and democratic theorists who were influential in establishing the principles for governance of this state—most explicitly Locke and Rousseau—adjunct to men and therefore their responsibility. While this adjunct position was considered an "esteemed" place, it rendered women invisible in the public arena.[10] In fact, the "invisibilizing" features of liberal democracy in the United States abrogate one of the fundamental tenets of liberalism: the idea that the individual's rights remain morally superior to the claims of the collectivity.[11] Willful obfuscation of this basic principle is at the heart of the argument for renewed attention to the definition of human being. Just what does it mean to confer certain kinds of rights on people? This question is especially critical in the absence of sufficient consideration of their standing prior to that conferral.

The term "civil rights" was not used until after the Civil War when abolitionists, fearing retribution by the former slaveowners on the freed slaves, pushed for legislation to protect them from abuse. The decision to legislate civil rights constituted an acknowledgment of the failure of the system to recognize all people as full citizens or as fully human. Yet, the enactment of civil legislation did not—in fact, could not—magically confer that humanness; neither does the enactment of legislation move back in time and adjust all the previously skewed standards to accommodate newly recognized humans. And, most importantly, as we have seen in the last few years, protections may be rescinded despite the absence of any real substantive change in conditions; simply because continued adherence is inconvenient. Civil rights are by their nature subject to the vagaries of politics; human rights are incontrovertible. Failure to recognize the rights of humans calls into question the legitimacy of the state. The question is not "are these beings human?" The question is rather, "is this state legitimate?"

As a sociopolitical condition of the conferral of civil rights, blacks and women were required to understand that they had done nothing to warrant the receipt of this bounty. They were in no case to see themselves as meriting these extraordinary efforts on their behalf. They had, therefore, to suffer with good grace the insinuations and outright claims as to their undeservedness. Since that time, the United States has moved, both temporally and psychologically, some distance from the source of its shame. Americans have become increasingly comfortable with disclaiming personal responsibility for discriminatory practices and, as a consequence, responsibility to alleviate the enduring burden. So, an inadequate remedy was instituted for the time that it took to recover from the collective discomfort engendered by people who supported ideological and cultural leaders like Sojourner Truth, Martin Luther King Jr., and Betty Friedan. That the remedy was inadequate, few question. Yet, because the measure was for some simply symbolic, for others a defense against anxiety, and for still others a necessary evil to keep the oppressed "from the door," the political will to find and institute a more appropriate remedy has always eluded Americans.

Nevertheless, the relevant question is not whether civil rights legislation corrects the enduring effects of differential status in the United States. It does not. The question to be answered is why, at the close of the twentieth century, in the United States of America, we have not found an acceptable, workable alternative to affirmative action.[12] On the contrary, we have simply moved far enough temporally from active abuse of human rights to warrant the denial of association with such abuse. That is to say that most exclusionary attitudes and practices are no longer actively malicious. Exclusionary practices are now simply unreflexively received truths. Today, continuation of the phenomenon "exclusion" requires little more than apathy. Yet, the prevailing belief is that in the absence of active oppression of others, what takes place will be normative, acceptable to all and will reveal the "truth" with reference to merit, status, and capacity. By claiming, at this point in the history of race relations in the United States, that we are a color-blind society, the Supreme Court gave tacit consent to dispense with efforts to ameliorate the injustices that still plague us. What we are faced with is an increasingly conservative Congress, a judicial system that is moving inexorably toward a gender-neutrality that threatens to obscure actual differences between men and women[13] and civil rights legislation that is under threat of rescission (legislation that has always been inadequately implemented, particularly for African Americans).

Conservative rhetoric around affirmative action invariably includes the terms "quota" and "reverse discrimination." In hiring practices and college entry processes, conservative rhetoric regarding quotas implies that a certain preset number of applicants of a particular characteristic will be accepted and that merit, as a criterion in applications, is at best irrelevant. Reverse discrimination implies that the mere coincidence of maleness and whiteness constitutes grounds for disregarding applicants bearing those characteristics. These terms are powerful and have justified, over the years, much of the most virulent resistance to civil rights legislation. Popular perceptions of a situation are severely delimited when the dominant argument is couched in such powerful, pejorative terms.

All the above attitudes and conditions serve to call into question the unequivocal commitment to human rights in the United States. As a result of this lack of commitment and despite the fact that early exclusionary practices have been modified over time, a differential status is maintained between full citizens and "others." Modifications of differences in access have taken the form of case law and civil legislation. Yet, case law, due to the generalization and application of particular decisions across differing populations and within varying circumstances, presents its own difficulties. Furthermore, attempts to confer rights through legislation fail because such legislation is enacted in substantial part to ameliorate the failure of the system to prepare excluded groups. Consequently, these "under-represented groups" were *by definition* unqualified. They had, then, to be afforded "special rights" and had to be given "undue preference."

The dialogue around civil legislation has always implied that the state was required to provide a false elevation to certain people until such time as they acquire the requisite qualifications to compete equally in the market. As a result, the popular view of women and African Americans as interlopers in the supposedly merit-driven world of paid labor, as "on the public dole," has become an intractable, social protocol. Their continued differential status and the temporary nature of remedies to that status is evident in the narrowness of the debate around (1) alternatives to affirmative action and (2) just what the "failure" of affirmative action means. Despite greater understanding of the inequities of the system, if one pays attention to the current debate over affirmative action, it becomes evident that little has changed in conservative discourse over the past 30 years. At its inception, affirmative action was seen as a temporary remedy instituted to salve the collective conscience of a complacent population grown slightly embarrassed by its relative prosperity. The peace marches and peaceful resistance of African Americans, particularly in the South, were delivered to an uneasy white America each evening with dinner.

But what are the implications of the differences between inherent human rights and conferred civil rights? Both the nature and the origin of specific rights carry with them very real effects. A civil right, when granted to citizens *in addition to* the inherent rights of human beings, constitutes a particular type of remedial action. This action is simply ameliorative—the correction of an oversight, if you will. On the other hand, when conferred upon a person whose humanness was previously undetermined or in any manner questionable, civil rights is another matter entirely. This second type of action makes the inaccurate assumption that civil and political rights constitute the full range of state provisions necessary to full citizenship. The assumption is further tested when one reviews the status of women in the United States in light of the definitions of human rights that are emerging in the world community. That differing conceptions of human being are entailed in human rights law as opposed to civil rights legislation becomes apparent: A human right implies that any system of government is unacceptable if it denies the full expression of the natural, inalienable rights of human beings. On the other hand, civil rights are merely adjustments to a systemic structure that is otherwise entirely acceptable. This is problematic especially if, as is the case in the United States, the system itself is structured around exclusion and oppression. Further, because the practice of exclusion is not simply civil and legal, but is also sociopolitical, economic, and cultural, more is required to alleviate these problems than civil remedies.

When women in the United States were granted civil rights, many believed that parity had been achieved along with more equalized access to the system. Yet, the reality remains that while women of all races, classes, and orientations and African American men have achieved nominal access, that access still, for example, has little effect on the institutionalized practices and processes that continue to privilege white, propertied males. Their newfound access also fails to penetrate the "networks" that exist between and among these white male elites. It is only in the light of the real distinction between civil equality and systemic equity that one sees, not just the inadequacy of a civil rights discourse to redress the preconditions for inequitable treatment, but the incapacity of a civil rights discourse to encompass questions of humanness. If the preconditions for inequity were not in place, would the question ever arise, for example, whether women are excluded from full compensation because they are women or if they are excluded because their work does not merit equal compensation?[14] What, exactly, are these preconditions?

First, given the failure of the system at its founding to recognize and honor the inherent human rights of some people, those people's rights—even their humanity—remained systemically undetermined. In the absence of human rights, those who were disenfranchised or marginalized necessarily appealed to the state to recognize their "civil" rights. The irony of the situation of "nonhumans" requesting civil recognition notwithstanding, social prejudices made the true realization of the rights subsequently granted virtually impossible. It became increasingly evident that granting formal rights that a system is unprepared to effect in social practice in itself constitutes an insufficient remedy. Civil rights discourse, to a large extent, disregards social and economic preconditions for unequal treatment and civil laws are certainly no substitute for inherent human rights.

Second, indicative in the "granting" of rights is the clear presumption that for some citizens those rights are not inherent. Moreover, the situation reaffirms that there exists a population for whom rights are inherent, a population who is in the position of granting or denying those rights to others. The act of conferring automatically establishes a differential status that is inextricably tied to the "unlike" characteristics of the human beings upon whom the rights are conferred. As a consequence, though *partially* redressed through civil rights legislation, marginalization and oppression of women and minorities in the United States was, and remains, a human rights violation.

One may, in reference to the history of race- and gender-based oppression in the United States, correctly note that conditions have improved, yet the distinction between formal equality and systemic equity remains at the heart of questions concerning U.S. interpretations of citizens' rights for all women. For example, despite legislation affording women control over their own bodies, we still debate whether women should be allowed to make decisions with regard to their own bodies. A very simple but telling example of both the continued ambivalence about women's control of their own bodies and men and women's differential status is the current debate over the substantially unquestioned insurance coverage of the new male potency drug Viagra juxtaposed with the decades of struggle to gain major health insurance coverage of the cost of birth control.

Third, a "radicalized" notion of state obligation would be that I, as "author" of the state would not form a system that denied my "location" within that same system. Yet, the prevailing notion of state obligation defines "full citizen" by standards and characteristics that apply to only a few inhabitants of the state, characteristics that "others" must attempt to emulate. Thus, a further problem with the attitude of granting, as in the case of civil rights, is the assumption that those who are thus afforded civil rights need only take on as best they can the characteristics of the extant privileged to be identified as full citizens. True equity is precluded by the underlying failure to recognize and value difference. Those who successfully replicate the attitudes and behaviors of the dominant elite may render themselves acceptable, but expression of self (and, more fundamentally, sense of self) is compromised.

All these limitations stultify creative growth in this country. This has been evident in the struggle of male, African Americans in the United States, but its complexities have been even more thoroughly exemplified in the struggles of women of all classes, races, sexual orientations, religions, and ethnicities. For example, women, given these constraints, would not allow their maternal status to become obvious, or worse, inhibit their performance in the workplace. Altering the conditions of work to accommodate "parental" responsibilities still, almost invariably, means "maternal" responsibilities. And the eventuality, or even the possibility, of "maternity" is still viewed as an obstruction to promotion.

Women are present in all dimensions of society, but they are recognized primarily by the state as serving "private" functions that are protected from state interference. This seemingly ineradicable social organization has caused many women to hesitate to expose themselves to what amounts to additional requirements that would be entailed by altered societal conditions. For those reasons and others, women themselves vary in their articulation of what is meant by their "rights." Some women have even begun to question whether a "rights discourse" constitutes the appropriate basis for remediation of their oppression.[15]

The need for civil legislation to provide even limited rights to women demonstrates the fundamental weakness in any argument that the United States is the embodiment of human rights and values. Nevertheless, the theoretical connection between liberalism and human rights law is the basis of U.S. claims to embody the values that human rights law represents. Assuredly, the foundations are similar, if not identical. The United States could, in fact, be a model for globalizing concern for human rights, simply on the basis of the fundamental consistency between natural law and liberal theory. Yet, the United States presents a troublesome model, as we have seen, in its application of the precepts of liberalism. One cannot successfully elide its systemic application of liberalism with the essential purposes of human rights law. International human rights law is clear that property right and human rights are not, and cannot be, limited exclusively to the few. Consequently, those few human beings who voluntarily contracted to enter the system at its founding, who assumed exclusive rights to own real property and other human beings in the United States and under U.S. laws, had no inherent right to be so exclusively privileged. What remains to be questioned is the continued corrigibility of the U.S. system.

The "idea" of a grantor-grantee relationship, that is assumed in the conferring of "civil" rights, is falsely based. Only the "idea" of human rights reveals the untenable assumption of the relationship. Ultimately, standing as a human being takes moral precedence over standing as a citizen. I am thus a human being, with all the moral autonomy the status entails, and only secondarily and consentually subject to the limitations of my location. Therefore the "idea" of human rights supercedes and displaces the "idea" of civil rights as insufficient, and replaces it with a conception of human rights to dignity and integrity that it is not within the legitimate power of the state to confer or deny. This displacement does not deny the sovereignty of the state with regard to international relationships nor does it eliminate the state's effective power. Rather, it holds the state to a moral standard that *already exists* if the state is a liberal democracy.

If the United States is to embody the ideals of human rights, it must reconsider its foundational myths and reconcile them with its historic realities. Enlightenment concepts of individuality (even the minds that formulated liberalism as a theoretical concept) did not conceive of human rights, but the rights of man in the most literal sense. Natural (human) rights are by no means limited to or strictly identified with atomistic, individualism. A culture that is founded upon these complementary concepts (that is, human and civil rights) is a culture that must provide for both continuity and change in its evolving social-legal order.

Finally, changes in the status quo are precluded by the unwillingness of the powerful to relinquish their political, economic, and psychological hold over the system. Therefore, it is not enough to argue the moral rectitude of such a critique. Investigating the ramifications of such pre-existing biases and questioning the legitimacy of their practical expression can only be further enhanced in dialogue with other states.

The grantor-grantee relationship that exists in terms of the *civil* rights of those who are marginalized by the U.S. legal, political, economic, and social systems undergirds my argument that the United States does not provide an unproblematic model in the globalization of concern for women's *human* rights. Though questions of legitimacy have arisen to challenge foundational interpretations and the responses to those questions have varied over time, they have found their ultimate expression in civil rights legislation.

Again, the argument here is not that unreflective ratification of mainstream human rights treaties would serve as a remedy to women's exclusion in the United States. The argument is that U.S. incorporation of mainstream international human rights principles and its involvement in the dialogue around advancement of those principles is a first step toward identification of women's human rights as a critical component of world peace and development. The further argument is that, subsequent to ratification of mainstream human rights instruments, ratification and incorporation of CEDAW would provide the conditions necessary to address, more adequately, the fundamental issue of women's "humanness."

One expects certain behaviors from a state that is founded upon, and claims to embody in its practices, human rights principles. And, as expected, relative to most other regimes, the human rights record of the United States is a reputable one. Yet, the United States has tended to position itself outside the international human rights discourse, and to exempt itself from the ratification process. Aside from its claims to embody human rights principles, the United States claims to have corrected any institutionalized practices of exclusion and marginalization of women through civil rights legislation. Assuredly, when the policy question is formed as one of access—a question of mere oversight or failure to fully accommodate—as has been the case in the United States, civil legislation would seem to be the appropriate relief. However, if one formulates the problem as one of denial of humanness and thus of citizenship itself, the solution is not so straightforward. The assumption in the U.S. system has been the former and the corollary assumption is that any remedy would necessarily be temporary.

In order to test those assumptions, one need only examine closely the theoretical underpinnings of U.S. founding principles and their practical expression within the system as it has developed. Such an examination reveals the inherent contradictions between both (1) the precepts of human rights and the underlying theoretical framework of the U.S. system, and then (2) the underlying theoretical framework of the U.S. system and actual practice in the United States. Therefore, due primarily to the particular application of theoretical premises in the formulation of founding principles and secondarily to the inadequacy of subsequent civil rights legislation as remedial to those early failures, the United States may not justifiably exempt itself from ratification of international treaties that protect human rights. In fact, using the words of Nietzsche, the forms that civil rights have taken in the United States are examples of "merely decorative culture."[16]

Within a liberal democracy, inherent, inalienable human rights ostensibly represent inviolable standards through reference to which the state is guided in its duty to all citizens. In the absence of unrestricted respect for those standards, state-conferred civil rights will constitute an insufficient remedy to oppression that predates, and thus has informed, the institutions of state. The existence of civil rights remedies in the United States, while encouraging, is not sufficient grounds to claim that the United States has reached a position where it may legitimately exempt itself from ratification and incorporation of international human rights instruments.

International Human Rights:
Redemptive or Redundant?

Women have been excluded from full citizenship under most governments and regimes and within most cultures of the world. With the advent of a global consensus on the value of human rights protections as an international alternative to reliance upon each state to recognize and protect human rights, one would assume that women were at last to be fully protected. Such is not the case. As the chapter title indicates, state refusal to recognize its own complicity in the enduring and pervasive violations of women's rights denies them access to protection under international human rights treaties. Violations of women's rights are not treated as human rights abuses, but rather as ordinary crimes. Even liberal democratic states fail to recognize and protect fully women's human rights. Unfortunately, the major international human rights covenants that emerged from that tradition extend only slightly beyond traditional protections in acknowledging the rights—even the existence—of women. Hence, the argument in the following pages that ratification of major international human rights instruments is a necessary, although not sufficient, condition to provide protection of women's human rights. The International Convention on Elimination of All Forms of Discrimination against Women (CEDAW) is the only international human rights treaty that provides comprehensive and explicit protections for women.

Global consensus around the need for collectively held standards in the area of human rights, though rhetorical in most cases, constitutes a positive direction in the world community. Therefore, as is the case in virtually all other nations of the world, the United States must come to terms with the need for reflection upon its own behavior with regard to violations that occur within its own borders. Contrary to popularly held belief in the United States, the liberal democratic system, as it has developed in the West, cannot be seamlessly elided with, nor can it be favorably compared to, the system of international human rights protections. U.S. refusal to ratify even the major human rights treaties, constitutes a failure of the United States to honor its commitments both to its own citizens and as a leader in the world community.

Why International Human Rights?

There are three fundamental questions to be asked in terms of international human rights protections and their effect on women: What is it that distinguishes international human rights protections from state protections? Why are international human rights protections necessary? What, if any, are the limitations of international protections? Although there are overarching principles that apply universally, specific answers to these questions remain relative to the system from which the questions themselves arise. The subject at hand is the U.S. system.

Liberal legal scholars would claim that there is very little if anything that distinguishes the precepts of liberalism from the fundamental protections of human rights. Theoretically, this is true. Nonetheless, for the United States, international human rights instruments are a reminder, in the face of contemporary legal, political, and socioeconomic systems in the United States, of the distortions in application suffered by liberal theory at this state's inception and in its subsequent development. Incorporation of international human rights instruments through the process of ratification would provide the United States the opportunity to "recover," in significant measure, fundamental theoretical liberal ideals by holding it responsible to aspire to those ideals for all of its citizens. Further, by virtue of contemporary realizations of the limits of American liberal foundational theories, the state is afforded the opportunity to reconstitute its notions of what it means to be human. Hence, the following argument is less about civil and legal treatment of citizens than it is about reconsidering the moral and ethical foundations upon which the state is premised in light of contemporary arguments as to its systemic and institutional limitations.

Why are international human rights protections necessary? In a liberal democratic state, the extralegal nature of human rights claims constitutes a reminder that the state has no choice in the matter of the existence of such rights, the state's only choice is whether it will establish and adhere to standards that reflect the existence of the rights. Granted, there are certain rights of human beings that may be beyond the economic means of a particular state to provide, for example, access to food or education. Within the context of a universal human rights regime, it is then the responsibility of the world community to ensure, to whatever extent possible, state fulfillment of structural obligations to human beings. Some responsibilities of the international community may entail economic support to the state, diplomatic sanction of certain practices by the state, or, alternatively, it may mean imposition of hitherto unrecognized responsibilities on the state.[17] Regardless of the specifics, it is the function of international human rights law to reassert the legitimate moral claims of the individual or group on the collectivity. Nonetheless, it remains the responsibility of each state to struggle to achieve equity.

One of the fundamental dilemmas of human rights law is that it asks universal and moral questions of particular politically and economically driven systems. Although it would be inaccurate to suggest that ratification of human rights treaties imposes strict, unavoidable standards upon the ratifying state, ratification of human rights treaties does constitute a pledge that is analogous to a statement of intent.[18] Again, for the United States, incorporation of human rights instruments represents less a reconstruction of existing legal standards than a moral re-ordering of priorities. Ratification by the United States would also reassert U.S. commitment to its responsibilities as a world leader.[19]

Following World War II, Western industrialized nations (particularly the United States) wielded significant influence in the creation of an International Bill of Human Rights (IBHR). The Universal Declaration of Human Rights (UDHR)—which is the document that sets forth the essential aspirations of IBHR—charges the international community with the provision of undifferentiated, universal protection for all human beings. As the provisions of the declaration were enumerated and made explicit in the two covenants that gave definition to its ideals—the International Covenant on Civil and Political Rights (ICCPR) and the International Covenant on Economic, Social and Cultural Rights (ICESCR)—it became increasingly evident that those definitions would necessarily be subjected to analysis through the lens of specific state agendas and traditional biases. Thus, the "idea" and the aspirations of human rights were limited in their application by the perceptions of a particular time and a particular set of human beings under very particular circumstances.[20] And each of the covenants encounters varied acceptance based, for example, on the geopolitical, economic, and religious conditions in each state or region.

For the most part, ICCPR does not challenge the limitations inherent to liberal democracy in the West: the default white, propertied male standard for full citizenship; the inviolability of the "private" space; and the definition of a human being as an autonomous individual. Conversely, ICESCR does extend beyond the traditional scope of Western liberalism as it was constituted in the late nineteenth and early twentieth centuries in that it requires states (1) to ensure a minimum standard of living to its citizens, (2) to respect the rights to self-determination of indigenous groups within the state's borders, and (3) to work toward providing a safe and clean environment. Yet, ICESCR does fail (albeit in a lesser way than ICCPR) to penetrate the traditional boundaries of privacy in a way that would allow it to extend its protections to women.[21] On that account, and despite current efforts to reconstitute the reporting procedures of ICESCR to make them more gender-sensitive, the International Convention on the Elimination of All Forms of Discrimination against Women (CEDAW) remains a necessary augmentation to these traditional, mainstream instruments.

For all the above reasons, concern for women requires the international community to move beyond simple examination of the limitations of state systems and structures and to ask the following questions about the current state of human rights protections: Does a gender-sensitive reassessment of the provisions of the IBHR challenge the parameters of human rights law? Yes. Does the same reinterpretation contradict the fundamental premises of human rights itself? No. The questions then are, if major "human" rights treaties do not include protection of the rights of women, what is the exact nature of their limitations? What does a category of women's international human rights entail and what are the implications of the need for such a category?

Women's Human Rights as a Legitimate Concept

Despite my earlier assertion that ratification of each of the covenants is essential, this does not mean to suggest that solutions to the problem of women's exclusion may be found through unreflexive recourse to international norms and standards in the form of IBHR. In fact, Hilary Charlesworth makes a compelling argument that this is not the case.[22] I do not even suggest here, for that matter, that true equity for women would be achieved through simple ratification of CEDAW. Although nonratification of CEDAW constitutes a critical failure of the United States in its duty to its citizens, ratification constitutes little more than a symbolic reaffirmation by the United States that citizens have rights that it are beyond the state's legitimate power to deny or retract and that those rights are universal. Ratification of CEDAW provides a framework for state provision and protection of the rights that women have not been in a position to exercise within most traditional state systems. Further, ratification with the intent to adhere unreservedly to the standards of CEDAW in a manner that requires global dialogue and allows for global scrutiny ensures a continued national dialogue that is critical to U.S. reassessment of its domestic and international responsibilities.

As human beings, we require more of ourselves when we come under the scrutiny of our fellows. This dynamic operates in personal interactions and at the level of international relations as well. In light of current political, social, and economic transitions around the globe, it behooves us—as an international community—to develop a relative consensus as to the nature of our shared aspirations. If we are to prepare the way for a peaceful and productive global future, then we must begin to require of ourselves the optimum in justice and fairness under common and reciprocal scrutiny. Preparing for the future means, precisely, recognizing current inadequacies and setting in motion processes to correct the inequities and shortcomings of the present. Women's international human rights has gained increasing attention over the last 20 years as a response to just such inequities and shortcomings.

The commitment to international human rights standards that is illustrated by involvement in the creation of the instruments and ultimate ratification of them is a positive goal for all states. Nonetheless, questions must invariably arise as to the efficacy of international instruments that were created by particular states during a time when those same states were themselves caught up in violent struggles around the idea of civil rights. Virtually all states at that time categorically denied women full citizenship. Thus, many of the limitations of mainstream human rights covenants are directly related to their emergence from and replication of limited conceptions of what constitutes citizenship. Thus, while ratification of mainstream human rights instruments constitutes a significant stride toward universal respect for human life, ratification remains an insufficient action in the attempt to rectify harms to those who have been, by definition, excluded from citizenship. At the same time, international human rights law does present a significant challenge to traditional international law and is a constant reminder, even to liberal states, of just what their responsibilities are to their citizenry. To appreciate both the challenge presented by human rights law and its limitations, one must be aware of the conditions from which the instruments emerged.

The proper subject of traditional international law was the state. The traditional relationship between and among states was based on respect for the sovereignty of each state,[23] which constituted a strong ethic of nonintervention. International agreements emerged from state-negotiated behaviors and practices that had been carried on over time and were considered "customary practice." In fact, states existed—and to a substantial degree still exist—in a natural, global anarchy in which all negotiation of terms is based on mutual cooperation and consent in the absence of an ultimate authority or a formal legislative body. Customary international law sprang from the perceived need to "regularize" activities that required interstate cooperation and was comprised of reflexive, mutually agreed upon standards. However, since the level of analysis in international relations was invariably the state, nothing within the state was a proper subject of international criticism. Simply stated, no action by the state within the state regarding domestic matters was open to international scrutiny. According to traditional international law, citizens only existed when they were abroad and then they were considered under the protection of their own state. Any violation of a foreign national's rights by a host government was an offense, not against the foreign national, but against his or her state. Under these conditions, the citizen whose rights were violated was the *cause* of an affront to their own government, not the respondent in the charge. Legitimacy to grieve (and power to redress) the wrong resided in the states, therefore, violations of citizens' rights by their own governments had no name. International human rights law gives these violations a name and, thus, constitutes a direct challenge to the traditional scope of international law.

As a phenomenon of the mid-twentieth century, and as a result of the atrocities committed during World War II, global recognition of crimes against humanity forced states to act in an unprecedented manner. The atrocities committed by the Third Reich against the Jews and other minorities, which far overstepped the boundaries of power that any artificially created governmental body could conceivably claim, forced the global community to recognize the need for international scrutiny of states' behavior toward their own citizens:

> The impact of the Second World War upon the development of human rights
> law was immense as the horrors of the war and the need for an adequate in-

ternational system to maintain international peace and protect human rights became apparent to all.[24]

International human rights law was established to ensure that individuals and groups would now have access to international protections and could make claims against their own governments. At long last, persistent and pervasive violations of citizens' rights that are (either explicitly or implicitly) perpetrated or permitted by a government or its agents were to be subject to sanction as human rights violations. Sanctions are justified because human rights violations are those violations that the state either refuses to or is incapable of remedying. If the claims made constitute legitimate human rights violations according to international human rights law, the world community is required to recognize the extralegal nature of these claims and to search for a remedy. However, in the event of such claims, UN correspondence on the subject is confined to legitimate agents of the state, thus, respect for the sovereignty of the state remains substantially intact. And, in the effort to remedy the abuse, the state is the correspondent of the relevant UN body.

Because international human rights law has been seen as an extension of the principles upon which Western liberal democracy is founded, one might assume that international human rights law has nothing to add to liberal ideals. Following that logic, one might argue that liberalism is fitting and proper for all contexts, or—the more modest claim—that within the particular context of the United States liberalism has found its optimum form. Yet, interpretations of liberalism were the work of eighteenth century philosophers who were constrained in their own ideas about what it is to be human. Further, the application of the founding principles continues to fall considerably short of the original conception of natural law. That shortfall has inevitably been reflected in international agreements.[25]

When, in the mid-twentieth century, representatives from various countries gathered to determine if the world could be redeemed by the formulation of a set of common and universal values, the proclamation of those ideals and values found its basic form in UDHR. UDHR remains an unexceptionable statement of the aspirations of the world community. Nonetheless, application of the ideal is always subject to interpretation. ICCPR and the ICESCR, which were offered for signature and ratification in 1966 and 1976 respectively, constitute those interpretations. ICCPR and ICESCR gave practical expression to the laudable aspirations that constitute the basis for preventing or, failing prevention, sanctioning identified crimes against humanity. Yet, those interpretations failed to address adequately the human rights of women.[26]

Debates still rage over interpretations and applications. Given the origin of human rights law, how is it possible to argue the superior capacity of international human rights protections to redress these conceptual limitations? In fact, no real remedy is found for women in the absence of CEDAW. This is not to say that ratification of the covenants is unnecessary. The covenants are invaluable. Certainly, their availability provides an international forum in which nongovernmental organizations (NGOs) may productively expand and develop women's agendas. However, their revolutionary nature and the importance of their interpretations notwithstanding, each of the covenants fails to address adequately violations of women's human rights.

Women and Human and Civil Rights in the United States: A Summary

In light of the failure of U.S. civil rights legislation to dislodge the enduring societal conceptions of women's appropriate roles, and given the perceived failure of affirmative action to achieve equity, the discussion inevitably turns to international human rights instruments. As the world community searches for definitions and struggles with systemic adaptations in the international discourse around human rights, there exists a "political space" within which to rethink priorities. Liberal democracy has been subjected to many and increasingly varied definitions that serve to fuel current rights debates. With due regard for the unexceptionable aspirations of liberalism as a concept, the argument here implicates liberal democracy, as it was defined and developed in the United States, in the marginalization and exclusion of particular human beings. Attempts, in the United States, to "reclaim" the virtues of liberalism through recourse to civil remedies have failed. Civil remedies fail to alleviate the oppression of African American men and all women in the United States precisely because civil legislation is delimited by a context. The context of civil legislation is one in which humanness is presumed already to have been established. Alternatively, human rights are preeminent. Human rights are those rights that exist as a result of a higher law than positive or man-made law. Such a higher law constitutes a universal and absolute set of principles governing all human beings in time and space. . . . associated primarily with John Locke, founded the existence of such inalienable rights as the rights to life, liberty, and property upon a social contract marking the end to the difficult conditions of the state of nature. This theory afforded recourse to a superior type of law and thus was able to provide a powerful method of restraining arbitrary power.[27]

However, at the founding of the United States, only propertied, white males had recourse to this "superior type of law." Women and slaves occupied an attenuated position: attached to legitimate, "full" citizens, yet not in and of themselves enjoying the freedom of participation. Neither could file lawsuits, nor could they enter into contracts, and therefore could not own property. Women could not demand remedy for even those things to which they were deemed entitled without male sponsorship. Women and slaves were subject to their husbands and owners and they were subject to the laws, but women and slaves had no influence in the legislative process nor were they party to the creation of the institutions that profoundly affected their lives.

Civil rights, by contrast to human rights, are those rights that the state confers upon citizens to *further* protect them from the state and others' molestation. Civil rights are then augmentary and supplemental and are conferred by the state after reflection upon the ways that the particular construction of the state might fail to address specific public intrusions into the private lives of its citizens. "Specific" meaning only those rights (1) precisely delineated and (2) of, or having, a public nature, because state "intrusion" in the private areas of life is prohibited in a liberal state. Not only women and "minorities" are provided access to the remedies and protections of civil legislation, but so are white, propertied males.

Any being included within the state and subject to state laws, yet not possessing the right to affect those laws must *necessarily* fail to meet—within that state's definition—either or both of the following criteria: (1) human and thus (2) citizen. If human rights are natural and inherent to all human beings and if they need not—in fact cannot—be conferred by the state, then all human beings must enjoy them. Yet, women and slaves in the United States, as the system was designed in the eighteenth century, did not meet those criteria. While this is no longer entirely the case, the methods and practices set in place to redress past inequities have been attacked as affording "special rights" and as being discriminatory toward white males. Yet, to eliminate these imperfect methods of redress without putting in place more appropriate remedies is to accept once again the default privileging of white males.[28]

Granted, the invisibility of women is more pronounced in many other countries than it is in the United States. Nonetheless, the systemic definitions of "citizen" in the United States and thus the violations that a citizen may suffer are circumscribed and limited to those violations suffered by the few who enjoy full citizenship. Close examination of the default male standard of full citizenship, which was epitomized by the public/autonomous actor, highlights the private/connected status ascribed to women: the private status that rendered women legally invisible and politically impotent. The advancements that women have enjoyed under case law have been for the most part salutary, but have not come without some negative effects. The tendency of the U.S. Supreme Court, and in many cases the lower courts, has been to view these cases very narrowly, using a standard that implies no difference between women and men. Because women's status has always been different from that of men, reliance upon this standard is particularly suspect.[29] While some liberal legal scholars have argued that parity may be achieved through access to equal rights, others argue that true parity involves also recognizing the distinctions between women and men. For example, Stetson claims that the contemporary movement in the U.S. legal system toward gender-neutral judicial interpretations, if realized, would

1. deny *actual* differences between men and women and between women themselves; and
2. fail, yet again, to penetrate the ideologically sustained boundaries between public and private areas of life.[30]

Thus, marginalization of women within the liberal democratic state is of a particularly subtle yet intractable nature.

Conclusion

Despite U.S. failure to recognize the human rights of all people, liberal democratic rights discourse concerning women in the late twentieth century in the United States continues to limit itself to emphasis on civil rights.[31] Judicial review of civil rights legislation has tended to narrow over time.[32] Further, civil rights legislation fails on at least two counts to redress violations of women's human rights: (1) its protections are supplemental and presume that the humanness of the subject is not in question; (2) its protections are public and therefore fail to penetrate the boundary of the private realm in which most harms to women occur. Civil legislation addresses the particularities of the culture within the context of the state system, that is, the ways in which the fundamental rights of full citizens within a particular state are augmented in an effort to ensure full and equal enjoyment of the protections of the state.

On the other hand, human rights are not delimited by contextuality and cultural relativity; they are, in fact, precontextual and see *only* humanness. Thus, they take precedence over and, ideally, inform the creation of the state. Those standards were edited considerably by the founders of the U.S. system. But, even if they got it wrong from the beginning, what does that say now? Is it too late to alter the conditions of people's lives? How can the United States respond to this dilemma? Does the topic at least warrant renewed debate?

When one juxtaposes the assumptions of liberalism with the reality of the U.S. systemic structure, it is evident that theory and practice diverge greatly. The psychological impact of that divergence on those who are marginalized is, alone, cause for alarm simply because their expectations are severely, if not entirely, curtailed. Granted, there are exceptions. Some people rise above their circumstances and achieve success by objective (though ill-defined) measures of success. There are others who squander their good fortune and fail to achieve even a modicum of success. But they are just that—exceptions. Also, the conditions of some lives are exceptional—either exceptionally bad or exceptionally good—and there are exceptional responses to those conditions. Ultimately, this discussion cannot be about the exceptions. It is finally necessary to ask questions about the common good, about the well-being of the unexceptional people who make up this country.

Chapter 2 🐍

The Convention on Elimination of All Forms of Discrimination against Women

Radical Notions of Human Being?

The full and complete development of a country, the welfare of the world and the cause of peace require the maximum participation of women on equal terms with men in all fields.[1]

—UN Treaty Series

The time has passed for isolated, remedial action by the state. Any effective remedy to the oppression of women is at this point in history, ultimately, an international one: a remedy that reaches into the private realm (or parallel state)[2] in which women are found globally and within which their particular harms are contained. The International Convention on Elimination of All Forms of Discrimination against Women (CEDAW), the most comprehensive treatment of women's international human rights in existence, is comprised of 30 articles that penetrate the traditional boundary between public and private areas of life and expose for remediation harms to women that have previously been denied full definition. Yet, the United States is among the few states that have not ratified the treaty.

There are various reasons why, despite its avowed commitment to freedom and equality, the United States has yet to ratify CEDAW. However, before examining U.S. behavior with regard to CEDAW, it is necessary to take a broader view of the behavior of the United States with regard to ratification of international human rights instruments in general—specifically the defining documents of the International Bill of Human Rights, the International Covenant on Civil and Political Rights (ICCPR), and the International Covenant on Economic, Social and Cultural Rights (ICESCR).[3] The purpose of a very broad look at U.S. behavior is to identify general—as opposed to treaty-specific—obstructions to ratification. Thus, the first section of this chapter provides a context within which to begin to assess U.S. non-ratification of CEDAW.

Contrary to popular assumption, the U.S. record on ratification of international human rights instruments is not an altogether positive one.[4] In fact, the propensity of the United States to avoid ratification of international human rights treaties is troubling on several counts. Without question, one would expect the United States to embrace most, if not all, human rights instruments. Yet, selective behavior on the question of human rights protections is nowhere more evident than in U.S. actions with regard to ratification of the defining documents of the Universal Declaration of Human Rights.

The United States ratified ICCPR in January of 1992, yet, has not ratified ICESCR. ICCPR requires, as the title implies, that a state provide its citizens the negative rights entailed within a (particularly Western) liberal democracy, that the state not intervene in private activities of its citizens, and that it also provide the structure for citizens' free expression of their will in preservation and operation of the laws of the land. ICCPR gives substantive meaning to Articles 3 through 21 of UDHR that "set forth the civil and political rights to which all human beings are entitled."[5] Again, provision of these rights is altogether consistent with the ideological basis of Western liberal democracy. Conversely, ICESCR emphasizes the rights that are of primary concern to preindustrial, non-Western, and third world countries: that the state provide such things as a standard of living adequate to health and well-being; that the state provide unimpeded access to education, the right to work, and so on. ICESCR gives substantive meaning to Articles 22 through 27 of UDHR that set forth the preceding and similar rights. Provision of these rights comes into significant tension with free market, liberal democratic ideals; their provision requires positive action and/or intervention by the state in what are in the West traditionally defined as private, political, or socioeconomic concerns. It is therefore not surprising that the United States ratified ICCPR, but has neglected to ratify ICESCR. In the neoConservative view, ICESCR (particularly in its focus on redistributive policies and economic rights) violates the fundamental basis of a liberal democracy that requires for its operation a market economy. ICCPR is, on the other hand, consistent with and establishes universal agreement concerning the rights upon which liberal democracy coexistent with a market economy is premised.

Both CEDAW and ICESCR continue to languish on the docket of the United States Congress. President Carter submitted CEDAW to Congress for advice and consent in 1980, and the International Convention on the Elimination of all Forms of Racial Discrimination, ICCPR, ICESCR in 1977.[6] No action has been taken on CEDAW or ICESCR—nor has any discussion of either treaty taken place—since the convening of the 104th Congress.[7] The case of each treaty serves a distinct and separate purpose in the following argument. Nonratification of ICESCR (as one of the interpretive documents of UDHR) raises questions about the particular definition of human rights in the United States and the relative importance of some rights as opposed to other, more readily derogated, rights. In fact, ICCPR so closely aligns itself with traditional liberal democracy in the United States that one is forced to wonder just how committed the United States is to an international dialogue. Finally, examination of U.S. behavior with regard to major international human rights treaties also provides a way of looking at U.S. foreign relations in general.[8]

ICCPR reinscription of the basic tenets of liberal democracy at the international level and ICESCR tension with market economic principles, however, are not the central issues here. Discussion of the two covenants in this chapter: (1) establishes the limits of the two covenants in their capacity to protect women and therefore the importance of the ratification of CEDAW, (2) provides a context within which to view the nature of U.S. (general) resistance to ratification of human rights treaties, and finally (3) argues the need to ratify both of the covenants regardless of their inherent limitations with regard to protection of women.

Mainstream International Human Rights Protections and Women

The assumption of women's equal status with men in the United States is just that, an assumption, with no basis in either social practice or in law. Further, this assumption of equality, coupled with the reality of male domination and state control, is in fact at the root of continued injustice to women in the United States. Consequently, fundamental international human rights instruments that reify traditional, liberal legal theory serve to reinstitute the marginalization of women within international human rights law.

Hilary Charlesworth outlines very clearly the failure of the International Bill of Human Rights to protect women against harms experienced solely on the basis of gender:

The development of human rights law has altered one set of boundaries between public and private in international law to allow the law to address violations of designated individual and group rights. This development however, has not challenged the much deeper public/private dichotomy based on gender: rights are defined by the criterion of what men fear will happen to them. As in domestic law, the non-regulation of the private sphere internationally legitimates self-regulation, which translates inevitably into male dominance.[9]

In her argument, Charlesworth examines each of the subsequent "generations" of rights and indicates how each explicitly avoids addressing harms that are peculiar to women. Her enumeration of those harms is as follows:

> From conception to old age, womanhood is full of risks: of abortion and infanticide because of social and economic pressure to have sons in some cultures; of malnutrition because of social practices of giving men and boys priority with respect to food; of less access to health care than men; of endemic violence against women in all states. Although the empirical evidence of violence against women is overwhelming and undisputed, it has not been adequately reflected in the development of international law. The great level of documented violence against women around the world is unaddressed by the international legal notion of the right to life because that legal system is focused on "public" action by the state.[10]

International bodies—including the United Nations itself—are composed of representatives of states that have traditionally discriminated against women. This fact in itself has served to limit remedial action within mainstream UN bodies.[11] Nonetheless, Celina Romany argues that the international community has a responsibility to hold states complicit in pervasive acts of violence against an identifiable group. As a precedent, she cites *Valesquez Rodriguez* v. *Honduras* (1989)[12] in which the state was held "complicit" in view of its continued failure to prevent disappearances and also failure to punish those responsible. She argues that, by this definition of complicity, endemic violence against women can also be attributed to the state by virtue of its failure to act:

> State complicity in "private" violations against women is not established by random incidents of non-punishment of violence against women, nor by merely equating approval of a particular crime with complicity in the crime, nor by arguing that non-punishment of a particular murderer amounts to complicity in the murder, nor relying on theories of derivative or remote liability or attenuated forms of responsibility. Complicity depends upon the verifiable existence of a "parallel state" with its own system of justice; a state which systematically deprives women of their human rights; a state which is designed, promoted and maintained by official state acts; *a state sanctioned by the official state* [emphasis mine].[13]

If state practices that exclude women are reinscribed and reified within international legal and political systems, women will continue to be marginalized despite state ratification of major international human rights treaties. In the United States the failure of the Equal Rights Amendment (ERA) provides an excellent illustration of the ambivalence surrounding women's rights even in a postindustrial liberal democracy. The notion that ratification of CEDAW is essential to the protection of women's human rights is significantly reinforced by such illustrations.

Because both ICCPR and ICESCR fail to penetrate the public/private boundaries that operate to exclude women from the creation and development of the instruments and institutions that affect their lives daily, CEDAW serves as a necessary and critical addition to the rights and protections afforded by the two covenants. The argument here is not that CEDAW in any way contradicts or detracts from the intent of the covenants. On the contrary, CEDAW offers a sound and nuanced augmentation of the covenants, thus providing women a remedy to the reductive tendencies inherent in Western liberal legal, social, and economic theories; tendencies that have been reinscribed by the fundamental mainstream international human rights treaties.

Women's Rights in the United States

The fact that the United States is among those states that have failed to ratify the treaty that would improve the situation of women within their own borders in itself provides just cause to question, if not the conceptual basis of the liberal democratic system, at the very least its implementation and the attitudes that prevail within this particular state. Susan James critiques the liberal democratic system in a virtual reiteration of the claim that Charlesworth makes against the international system. James says, concerning the liberal democratic state,

> The theory and practice of democratic liberalism are much criticized at present on the grounds that they exclude women from full citizenship. They do this in two ways: by denying women the full complement of rights and privileges accorded to men, and, more insidiously, by taking for granted a conception of citizenship which excludes all that is traditionally female. The cluster of activities, values, ways of thinking and ways of doing things which have long been associated with women are all conceived as outside the political world of citizenship and largely irrelevant to it.[14]

Despite the accuracy of this critique, if the liberal democratic system were not improvable and had no potential for inclusion of all citizens, there would be no reason to carry out this study. It is the very corrigibility of the system to which this critique addresses itself.

The basis for international human rights claims is found in the Western, liberal ideology of freedom, equality, and the individual rights that are morally superior to the claims of the collectivity. The rights provided in ICCPR are equivalent to those basic "negative" rights provided in Western liberal democracy. Even ICESCR provides no assurance of equal access to economic "goods" beyond those which would be available within a strong welfare state. Yet, debate in the United States, however limited, centers around the inadvisability of the ratification of ICESCR. Consequently, it is not the tension that exists between traditional liberal democratic ideals and ICESCR that is problematic within the context of my argument. The issue is the virtual agreement of both ICCPR and ICESCR with the liberal democratic ideals of the United States. Each of the covenants restricts its protections almost entirely to the rights of the citizen with regard to public relationships. For example, ICESCR protects the right to work and the right to a living wage as opposed to the requirement to recognize women's contributions—in the private arena—that have not been compensated.[15]

Women realize rights and freedoms under the U.S. liberal democratic system that would not be available to them in many other countries of the world. Of course, this does not mean that the freedoms that American women enjoy were available to them within the original structuring of the system. Nor does it mean that American women today enjoy rights in the same way as do white males within the same system. It does mean, however, that women do enjoy relative political and economic access in most Western cultures. That women enjoy such political and economic access is a tribute to the corrigibility of the liberal democratic system, as well as to the decades of struggle by women to attain some measure of equity. Yet, this very same liberalism—as it has been defined and practiced in the West—continues to fail, in a fundamental way, to address the harms suffered by women and others who do not fit the traditional description of "full citizen."[16] Therefore, women have continued the struggle to define and implement strategies that would afford them equal social and legal status with men. Unreflective reference to the white male standard in determining excellence has proved detrimental to the process of inclusion of women—as women. Not surprisingly, the "equality" that women have achieved has been granted them by virtue of their capacity to replicate male characteristics and behavior. This "equality" has been granted solely in the public space despite strong empirical evidence that equality in the public space has little ameliorating effect on the particular harms that women suffer because they are women. The real harms that women suffer occur in the nebulous area of the private space—the private space that is protected in a liberal democracy by virtue of citizens' negative rights against interference by the state. Nevertheless, in the 1970s women continued to believe that legal equality with men was the answer.

In the late 1970s, the United States was on the verge of ratification of the Equal Rights Amendment to the Constitution, which would grant women equal status with men. Though it was approved by a two-thirds vote in Congress, ratification of the amendment was not supported by the requisite number of states, and on June 30, 1982, the effort failed.[17] With regard to the critical necessity for such an amendment and the dire implications of its failure to pass, Jane Pickering warned in 1977:

> Since the Equal Rights Amendment would provide a vehicle for attack upon any governmental policy which might be discriminatory in nature, its importance cannot be underestimated. Legislation can be repealed more readily than can a constitutional amendment. Failure of the ratification effort would dim the hopes of women throughout the country of achieving legal equality, and also would give rise to concern for the survival of the gains already achieved.[18]

What Pickering did not say was that equality, given women's different location within the social structure, was a far cry from justice. Equality within the structure as it was designed denies actual differences in the situations of men and women. As Adriana Cavarero reminds us:

> It is possible to be both different and equal, if each of the two different beings is free and if the kind of equality at stake radically abandons any foundation in the logic of abstract, serializing universalization of the male One. It is possible to be both different and equal if not only a new logical foundation of the concept of equality can be developed, but a new model of society and politics.[19]

With those caveats in mind, Dorothy McBride Stetson argues (contrary to Pickering) that the contemporary movement in the U.S. legal system toward gender-neutral judicial interpretations, if realized, would deny actual differences between men and women and fail to penetrate the boundaries around the private lives of women.[20]

The implication of the tension between the arguments of Pickering and Stetson, the failure of the ERA, and the radical notions of society provided by Cavarero is that women themselves differ greatly in their perceptions of marginalization and the particular actions necessary to remedy that marginalization. Many of the arguments by women against ratification of the ERA centered around the possible negative consequences for women of such a move. To the two problems seen by Stetson, I would add a third. There was considerable room for speculation about the practical application of the broad, ill-defined terms of the amendment. In the initial attempts to gain support for ratification and the subsequent interpretations of the amendment itself, the system as it existed at the time and the cryptic wording of the amendment operated in concert to defeat ratification. In that sense the failure of ERA was one of inference: The debate factionalized what had appeared, initially, to be strong public support. Cavarero's point, then, is well taken. A "new model of society" is necessary to begin the process of recovery.[21]

These inherent flaws would be avoided in the ratification of CEDAW: (1) it does *not* deny actual differences in lived experience; (2) it does penetrate public/private boundaries; and (3), considering the thorough and rigorous delineation of the protections it provides, CEDAW would not allow such unlimited space for conjecture. Further, ratification of CEDAW in the wake of ratification of ICESCR would provide a common global language in service of an increasing sense of world community.

What Are the Possible Effects of Ratification?

C. B. MacPherson, in his *The Life and Times of Liberal Democracy,* notes in passing that because women, as a group, do not constitute a "social class" their rights have been abrogated with impunity.[22] There being no other reference in his text to the phenomenon, one could assume that for MacPherson the statement sums up the problem. Of course, there are other less obvious factors at work, but MacPherson does make an important point, however cursory his attention. Because they lack functional commonalities that constitute (among other things) a class, women have had to remain conscious of the importance of embracing distinctions of class, race, ethnicity, and sexual orientation in order to achieve the gains they have. What, then, is the most effective way to address the seemingly ineradicable discrimination that women face? U.S. ratification of CEDAW is critically important for two fundamental reasons—one domestic and the other global. First, if the U.S. judicial system is, as Stetson argues, on the verge of opting for gender-neutral language as a response to women's continued marginalization, then incorporation of CEDAW would provide practical guidelines for consideration of just what legal equality should entail.

> To use law as an effective strategy in the feminist struggle for gender equality requires changing the male perspective embedded in law; and, in turn, this requires women's voices. But women's voices are barely audible against the backdrop of patriarchal legal traditions, institutions, processes, and statutes. Adding women to a male legal process makes little difference unless it is connected to broader feminist struggles for social change.[23]

Second, U.S. ratification of ICESCR and CEDAW would offer the United States greater opportunity for a more thorough involvement in global dialogue.

> If the United States keeps itself apart from these regimes, as it has done on the core human rights regime, it will not be able to exercise much leadership on the multilateral dimension of global human rights. Even other democratic states, which normally cooperate with or defer to U.S. leadership, like Sweden and the Netherlands, will learn to act without the United States as they did with regard to the convention on torture.[24]

In the past several years an increasing number of states have moved toward implementing liberal democratic systems of governance. As a world power, the United States could provide a model for emerging democracies. However, before the liberal legal, political, and economic systems in the United States can be expected to serve as a positive universal model for the alleviation of women's oppression, its commitment and effective involvement in the contemporary movement toward global interdependence and common purpose must be made evident. Only then can the liberal legal, political, and economic systems be (potentially) relied upon to illuminate and address women's exclusion.

The following analysis explicates the specific purpose of each article in part 1 of CEDAW. The actual structure of the convention describes a necessary and specific movement from very abstract and generally accepted premises into the depths of the "dark corners" of women's lived experiences. The experiences of women have been invisibilized by traditional cultural and social constructs, political norms, and legal standards in virtually every nation of the world. Consequently, the strictures of the convention force an interrogation of traditional norms and standards, and require each state party to assume an active role in eliminating and/or mitigating the gender-based inequitable treatment of its citizens. Moreover, CEDAW carefully outlines both general and specific remedies for the systemic inequities and oppressive societal biases that have limited women's participation and equal operation within each state. However, the attitudes within the UN are in no manner disjunctive with the attitudes that prevail within specific states—a situation that effectively compounds the problem. The UN itself is composed, almost entirely, of male representatives. As a result, analysis of CEDAW is an appropriate precursor to the identification of the failures of the liberal legal and liberal democratic systems from which human rights protections stem. The analysis illustrates the reinscription by major international human rights treaties of the public/private boundaries that serve to invisibilize women.

CEDAW is the subject of this analysis because it is the first international document offered for state ratification that deals directly and comprehensively with the status of women globally. As a result of its specificity, CEDAW has suffered more substantive reservations than other international conventions—even other human rights conventions.[25] CEDAW has encountered such resistance—both at national and international levels—as a direct response to its exclusive focus on women's oppression.

Continued state resistance to rectifying women's unequal status is based on the assumption that maintenance of women's traditional roles is integral to (1) the economic stability of the state, (2) the emotional, psychological, and nutritional health of children, (3) the education and socialization of children, and (4) maintenance of the family (as the principle organ of social order). Consequently, according to CEDAW's detractors, the incorporation of women's human rights (and the subsequent alteration of the conditions of their oppression) would pose a fundamental threat to the stability of the state, the welfare of its children, and the privacy afforded the nuclear family. Such is not the case. Despite the "disarray" (some would say chaos) caused by the incorporation of women's rights into state systems, if commitment to liberal democratic ideals is a primary goal of the state, then adherence to the basic precepts of liberalism is a requirement for the realization of that goal. The welfare of the world and its peoples is dependent upon the inclusion and free expression of all citizens as full participants in the institutions and organs that affect their lives. Yet, actual commitment to such goals has been absent, not only in the operation of "lesser" regimes, but in the practical application of liberal democracy in the United States. It is therefore not surprising that full commitment to women's human rights has also been absent in human rights treaties that supposedly focus on women.

CEDAW differs from other women's rights conventions in that it is a comprehensive instrument and, additionally, focuses on the violation of women's human rights without the stultifying and inhibiting modifications in wording that have been included in previous international treaties. Such modifications have been incorporated in the past due, primarily, to the prevalent, though tacit, understanding that women's human rights are derogable. The enduring assumption within states is that the recognition of women's human rights undermines the political, economic, and cultural stability of the state. This assumption remains operative despite compelling evidence to the contrary and, therefore, forces one to question the actual basis for women's oppression.[26] Further, if the stability of a liberal democratic state is in fact contingent upon systematic derogation of the rights of a particular sector of society, then the legitimacy of that state *must* come into question. The same may be said for attempts to sustain any repressive social order.

The preservation of religious practices and customary traditional/conventional social orders—the fundamental interest of which is the stability of the nuclear family—have continued to take legal and moral precedence over the protection of women's human rights in the United States. Derogation of women's human rights to the interests of the state constitutes a basic and immediate denial of women's humanity, in terms of liberal theory, upon which human rights are premised.[27] Over time, attempts to protect women have taken various forms. Most of the attempts have had as their base some idea of state interest in women's primary functions.

Natalie Hevener, in *International Law and the Status of Women*,[28] sets forth three analytic categories that are helpful in describing the range of protections that have been available to women. They range from stultifying to liberating and in specific contexts reinforce particular assumptions about women. In her analysis, Hevener also constructs a thorough, historic analysis of the international instruments that have been designed to address the subordination of women. The following categories form the basis of that work:

1. *protective conventions:* essentially sustain traditional ideas of women's "subordinate status": their inability to make "rational decisions about their own lives"; their need to be protected through "completely proscribing or restricting their participation in certain areas of activity";

2. *corrective conventions:* deal primarily with the gross mistreatment of "women" as a very specific category, implying that "men are not involved as victims," in that such corrective measures deal directly with isolated, specific incidences of mistreatment of women. Rarely do these conventions deal with the larger facilitating (at best) and proscribing (at worst) social context in which the mistreatment occurs; and

3. *nondiscriminatory conventions:* attempt "to revise the legal system in such a way that sex will no longer be a basis for the allocation of benefits and burdens in society."

Mixed conventions are those which include within their provisions some or all of the foregoing categories. CEDAW is an example of what Hevener refers to as a "mixed convention."

The following analysis illustrates a number of ways that ratification of CEDAW might highlight the pervasive, transhistoric obstructions to the recognition and protection of women's human rights in the United States. There is a disjuncture between de jure and de facto treatment of women. This disjuncture is evident in U.S. political, legal, and social systems. That the disjuncture exists in the United States further emphasizes the fact that oppression and invisiblization of women occurs, not simply within states that have normally been viewed as oppressive, but in socially and techno-logically "advanced" Western liberal democracies. Therefore, the articles of CEDAW that are highlighted here are those that call into question tradi-tional legal, political, and societal norms in the United States. The analysis represents an initial step toward (1) assessing the shortcomings of the liberal democratic system as conceived and developed in the United States and (2) proposing positive changes in national and international fora in order to make possible women's full participation. Accordingly, the following section sets out part 1 of CEDAW. The entire document is presented in the appen-dix of the text. Part 1 constitutes a general overview of the more specific parts of the convention, so lends itself to a general investigation of the U.S. system relative to women's international human rights.

The Convention on Elimination of All Forms of Discrimination against Women.

The United Nations General Assembly adopted CEDAW on December 18, 1979, after five years of consultations with the Commission on the Status of Women (CSW) and various working groups. Prior to adoption of the con-vention, there existed several major international documents that made broad reference to women's human rights. Among them are: The United Na-tions Charter; The Universal Declaration of Human Rights; The Interna-tional Covenant on Civil and Political Rights; The International Covenant on Economic, Social, and Cultural Rights; and the American Convention on Human Rights. Though these documents referred to the rights of all human beings, there was no particular focus on violation of human rights that are peculiar to women simply because they are women. Thus, harms to women remained invisible. They had not traditionally been exposed for ex-amination by state systems and were, subsequently, not made present by these mainstream documents.[29] What is more, when the documents were subjected to gender-sensitive critiques, they were found, in many cases, to undermine women's rights. Therefore, in addition to the aforementioned documents, treaties were drafted that dealt specifically with the protection of the legal rights of women: The International Convention on the Political Rights of Women; The Inter-American Convention on the Granting of Po-litical Rights of Women; the international labor conventions; and conven-tions dealing with the nationality of women, marriage, white slavery, and prostitution. These specific documents are what Hevener names "corrective" in that they dealt directly with one, or a small number of, specific abuses of women's rights. Furthermore, all the documents mentioned above deal ex-clusively with the "public" relationships in which women engage. Not until CEDAW was drafted and offered for ratification was there a document that addressed the human rights of women in a comprehensive manner. Prior to the drafting of CEDAW, the "private" conditions of women's lives had been exempted from inspection by formally binding documents. Even the wording of the nonbinding Declaration on Elimination of All Forms of Discrimination against Women (DEDAW), the signature of which preceded the drafting of CEDAW, was less than satisfactory. In fact, the clause that was required by the United Nations General Assembly before DEDAW could be offered for signature is found in Article 6(1) and is worded as follows:[30]

> *Without prejudice to the safeguarding of the unity and the harmony of the family,* which remains the basic unity of any society, all appropriate measures, particularly legislative measures, shall be taken to ensure to women, married or unmarried, equal rights with men in the field of civil law. [emphasis mine]

This preemptive regard for the integrity, unity, and stability of the family and the reference to civil law virtually guaranteed the impossibility of reaching women within the confines of the private realm. Thus, the unmitigated wording of CEDAW constitutes both an increased awareness of women's location and a positive move in the direction of real protection of their human rights.

Because the harms that women suffer are primarily experienced within the private realm that includes—but, is by no means limited to—the family, CEDAW was literally lifesaving for women. This is not to say that the traditional nuclear family is an entirely undesirable institution. Rather, CEDAW serves to underscore the fact that the state is responsible for safeguarding the basic human rights of women as well as men. The convention, therefore, questions the legitimacy and provides for the alteration of any public or private structure, institution, or practice that disregards or infantalizes women. It is increasingly evident that, rather than remaining bound by a priori consideration of the negative rights of full citizens, states must be willing to take positive action to alter conditions that govern such exclusion.[31] The following analysis highlights those conditions.

Again, the full text of CEDAW is located in the appendix to this text. Part 1 of CEDAW, with commentary, is included within the text because it constitutes an overview of the requirements dealt with more specifically in later parts of the convention.

Part 1

Article 1

> *For the purposes of the present Convention, the term "discrimination against women" shall mean any distinction, exclusion or restriction made on the basis of sex which has the effect or purpose of impairing or nullifying the recognition, en-*

joyment or exercise by women, irrespective of their marital status, on a basis of equality of men and women, of human rights and fundamental freedoms in the political, economic, social, cultural, civil and or other field.

This article challenges the message, implicit in domestic as well as international law, that although women are (for the most part) considered human beings, there is a real and present difference in the legal/moral status among citizens that clearly breaks down along gender lines. This distinction, which continues to exist in domestic law as well as cultural and societal norms, has been reinscibed in international law, and so must be eliminated. The debate around issues of gender raises questions in relation to the following: (1) the responsibility of international bodies in states' behavior with regard to the public/political recognition of the "citizen"; (2) the responsibility of the state with regard to public/private actions of citizens; and (3) the possibility of international and state responsibility in the private actions of individuals and collectivities. These issues describe a particular hierarchical structure: those that are of international concern, those within the auspices of state authority, and those governed by private individual or collective choices.

Women have traditionally inhabited the third dimension of this hierarchical framework (that is, the domain in which private actions of individuals and collectivities are the prevalent moral force). Women's location within the "private realm" is ostensibly protected from interference by the government or any other "public" organ, thus any harms they might experience within that realm are rendered invisible and therefore invoke no public responsibility. Given these conditions, women live as virtual aliens within their own states.[32]

Article 2

States Parties condemn discrimination against women in all its forms, agree to pursue by all appropriate means and without delay a policy of eliminating discrimination against women and, to this end, undertake:

(a) To embody the principle of the equality of men and women in their national constitutions or other appropriate legislation if not yet incorporated therein and to ensure, through law and other appropriate means, the practical realization of this principle;

This subsection clearly requires those states that choose to include gender equity as a value within their legal systems to establish as a foundation not only constitutional measures, but also, when necessary, states are required to define more clearly the requirements of said constitution through legislative enactments. Consequently, laws that have traditionally been unable to reach women in the private realm must be accompanied by "other appropriate means" to accomplish true equity—not simply in opportunity but in access, not simply de jure but also de facto equity. These "means" include positive action taken by the state to alter traditions and conventional behaviors that have historically denied women true access to institutions and positions that have direct impact on their lives. Accordingly, the realization of equity requires states to eliminate inherent systemic inequities and offer marginalized groups unequal support until such time as past systemic inequities have been redressed.

(b) To adopt appropriate legislative and other measures, including sanctions where appropriate, prohibiting all discrimination against women;

This subsection requires states to give appropriate emphasis to citizens' adherence to altered traditions and conventional behaviors that have unfairly discriminated against women. When necessary, states are enjoined to take punitive action if such strictures are disregarded.

(c) To establish legal protection of the rights of women on an equal basis with men and to ensure through competent national tribunals and other public institutions the effective protection of women against any act of discrimination;

Recognizing that legal measures without appropriate and sufficient enforcement bodies are impotent, this subsection adjures states to establish or modify such institutions when necessary in order that they may realize the capacity to carry out the strictures found in Article 2(a), and to adjudicate actions inconsistent with these strictures, whether by individuals or collectivities, that tend to deny women their rightful status—once that status is constitutionally established.

(d) To refrain from engaging in any act or practice of discrimination against women and to ensure that public authorities and institutions shall act in conformity with this obligation;

Once established or modified, such organs of the state must, according to this subsection, be monitored by the state in a rigorous effort to ensure the complete protection of women's rights. The state is recognized by this subsection as fully responsible for the accomplishment of goals found in Article 2(c).

(e) To take all appropriate measures to eliminate discrimination against women by any person, organization or enterprise;

This subsection emphasizes the responsibility of the state beyond its own behavior and the actions of state organs. The state must use all necessary diligence to ensure that appropriate measures are carried out by all agents and organizations—whether public, private, or individual—that have the capacity to discriminate against women.

(f) To take all appropriate measures, including legislation, to modify or abolish existing laws, regulations, customs and practices which constitute discrimination against women;

This subsection requires the state to take the responsibility of advising all public or private entities in the practical application of principles of nondiscrimination as they pertain to women. Adherence to this article may require states to undergo a comprehensive analysis with the purpose and intent of reviewing legislation and rewriting policies that discriminate unfairly against women.

(g) To repeal all national penal provisions which constitute discrimination against women;

Finally, the state must rid its civil penal codes of all wording that may lead to, result in, or require discrimination against women or, conversely, disregard the equal responsibility of women.

Article 3

States Parties shall take in all fields, in particular in the political, social, economic and cultural fields, all appropriate measures, including legislation, to ensure the full development and advancement of women, for the purpose of guaranteeing them the excerise and enjoyment of human rights and fundamental freedoms on a basis of equality with men.

This article commits the state to affirmative action in redressing traditional and/or conventional exclusion of women from involvement in or access to public and private forms of organization in the aforementioned areas that hold sway over, regulate, or otherwise unduly influence their social and/or productive activities.

Article 4

1. Adoption by States Parties of temporary special measures aimed at accelerating de facto equality between men and women shall not be considered discrimination as defined in the present Convention, but shall in no way entail as a consequence the maintenance of unequal or separate standards; these measures shall be discontinued when the objectives of equality of opportunity and treatment have been achieved.

Article 4, in recognition of the unequal measures that may be necessary to eradicate fundamental disregard and/or inherent discrimination against women, does not name the unequal measures "discrimination" in that the measures are self-conscious efforts serving specific, agreed upon purposes. Consequently, once judged effective in the eradication of systemic inequities, such measures shall be discontinued.

2. Adoption by States Parties of special measures, including those measures contained in the present Convention, aimed at protecting maternity shall not be considered discriminatory.

Maternity is by its nature uniquely the purview and capacity of women. As such, it shall be protected as inherent to their own bodies and is not to be considered a matter or function over which others may hold primary dominion or undue preemptory influence.

Article 5

States Parties shall take all appropriate measures:
(a) To modify the social and cultural patterns of conduct of men and women with a view to achieving the elimination of prejudices and customary and all other practices which are based on the idea of the inferiority or the superiority of either of the sexes or on stereotyped roles for men and women;

Each state is required to institutionalize educational and vocational processes and to reinforce and support grassroots efforts whereby arbitrary distinctions based on sex are eliminated and both sexes are encouraged and prepared to realize their potential in whatsoever roles, areas, or functions they choose—limited only by actual aptitude or capacity.

(b) To ensure that family education includes a proper understanding of maternity as a social function and the recognition of the common responsibility of men and women in the upbringing and development of their children, it being understood that the interest of the children is the primordial consideration in all cases.

Though women are uniquely biologically capable of conceiving and producing children, the state must actively involve itself in creating social awareness as to the very real common responsibility of parents of both sexes in childrearing, in that social—not biological—distinctions have ascribed the task of childrearing to the mother and/or other females.

Article 6

States Parties shall take all appropriate measures, including legislation, to suppress all forms of traffic in women and exploitation of prostitution of women.

Neither the company nor the sexuality of women shall be controlled by anyone other than themselves—for profit, influence, or any other social, political, or economic "good."

United States' Record on Women's Rights: Why Ratify CEDAW?

None of the articles of CEDAW is entirely inconsistent with the fundamental bases of liberalism. Yet, the United States has refused to ratify CEDAW for over a decade. One argument for nonratification of both ICESCR and CEDAW is that the operation of the market does not allow for legal assurances of a minimum standard of living, much less access to the system to those who are not considered full citizens. Nevertheless, in the period since the end of World War II, the United States has been forced to struggle against an ever-increasing pressure to replace the state-passive concept "equal opportunity" with the state-active assurance of equal access—a goal that requires positive action by the state for its realization. Equal access, as a standard, is in substantial tension with the operation of a "free market." The corrective measures necessary to provide equal access violate, by some accounts, the fundamental connection between individual (negative) rights against state intervention and competition within the protected space of private enterprise.

According to Leslie Calman, it is therefore not surprising that international claims to rights to food, subsistence wages, and health services first found voice in non-Western and third world states that were struggling toward a new socioeconomic world order. The claims made by these struggling peoples represented a reversal of the priorities that had traditionally dominated Western political thought:

> In the early nineteenth century the earlier normative emphasis on the rights of individuals, natural rights, and rights against the state shifted to a belief in rationalism, secularism, and humanism. Socialist thinking challenged the moral primacy of the individual and placed new emphasis on the importance of the community. Socialism also questioned the value of political rights in the

absence of economic sufficiency; government was understood to be not an institution from which individuals should demand benign neglect, but one responsible for the welfare of its citizens.[33]

Would such a reordering of economic (public) priorities *necessarily* have a salutary effect on women? What does this tension mean in terms of women's human rights? What are the implications of refocusing economic priorities, for women?

Liberal democracy has been the basis of the American system of governance for over two hundred years. The challenges encountered over the last two centuries have sometimes divided but, overall, have strengthened the social and political fiber of the country. In confronting the challenges facing women, grassroots and other emergent groups—the very essence of democratic society—came together on critical substantive issues and continue to effect change within existing processes and institutions. The task has been an arduous one given the existence of thoroughly engrained systemic proclivities. Of course we may theorize about utopia: The potential perfection of the system is a tantalizing dream. But it is ultimately the process—the "muddling through" within a preset context—that describes the human condition.

The socially ascribed role of women has traditionally been that of homemaker and caregiver within the private realm of society. The Constitution, subsequent legislation, and most case law developed in the United States with that ascription as a basic, unquestioned premise.[34] Specific circumstances notwithstanding, that ascription remains a default legal, political, social, and economic reality common to women. So, despite her relative achievement (or lack of achievement) in the "public space," a woman encounters specific resistances to recognition of any "unusual" circumstances (that is, circumstances outside her constitutionally, socially, and politically ascribed role). Evidence that these issues remain unresolved is found through reference to the litigation necessary to establish—for a woman—the rights expected, without question, by her male counterpart.

Two situations that illustrate the ways these unresolved issues affect women are: (1) a young, unmarried mother on welfare and (2) an economically successful woman being denied her de facto position as head-of-household.

Stetson describes the situation of women in this way:

A person's economic status is closely related to his or her earning power and employability. For women, employability has been limited not only by inadequate vocational and job training, child-care responsibilities, and family dependence but also by the culture, which has not defined women's roles in terms of autonomy and self-sufficiency. Being economically responsible for oneself and one's family has been officially defined as the exception for women, but the rule for men.[35]

The first part of Stetson's argument applies to situation one, and the second part to situation two.

The first type of discrimination is commonplace and well-documented, so requires little explication.[36] The situation, as it is described, implicates the state in its failure to counter the detrimental effects of a system that rigidly proscribes—and operates on the assumption of—oppressive and marginalizing gender roles without due consideration of actual circumstances.

The situation of the second woman provides a counterpoint from which to view the phenomenon of women's exclusion. Despite a woman's economic (public) circumstances, in the absence of litigation the legal system (and virtually all other state institutions) continues to assume a dependent position for her in relation to her husband. The system is unable to accommodate the particular circumstances of women's lives.

In *Frontiero* v. *Richardson* (1973), the U.S. Supreme Court found it unconstitutional to require that a husband prove that half his support came from his wife before he could be claimed as a dependent. There is no such requirement of proof necessary for a wife to be claimed as a dependent. The question here is not whether the Supreme Court's decision was equitable, the point is that the case reached the U.S. Supreme Court at all. Application of the strict test "suspect classification" was not necessary in this case because the lower court decision failed to meet even the lesser standard of ordinary scrutiny.

Yet, gender is still not considered a "suspect classification."[37] If gender were considered a suspect classification, many of the cases now being litigated might be rendered irrelevant. Legal interpretations by the lower courts, while in many cases the purview of the state, rely heavily on U.S. Supreme Court decisions for guidance. A good decision is one that will stand if appealed to the higher court. Yet, with the failure of the Equal Rights Amendment in 1973, the Supreme Court is wary of using the stricter test. According to Stetson,

> Thus far, the effect of the Supreme Court's "judicial notice" of the differences between men and women has tended not to challenge but rather to reinforce traditional stereotypes about women's economic dependency (*Kahn* v. *Shevin*), sexual behavior (*Michael M.* v. *Supreme Court of Sonoma County, CA*), and parental roles (*Parhnham* v. *Hughes*). The problem is that these differences are defined by male judges from a traditional, male legal perspective.[38]

Romany's assertion of the "verifiable existence of a parallel state" is substantially borne out in virtue of these situations.[39]

Conclusion

It should be a compelling interest of the state to ensure equal treatment of its citizens *or* it should be a compelling interest of the state to support fully those who occupy a position defined by the state as dependent—who, yet, provide a service that is integral to state purposes. It should not be a compelling interest of the state to maintain a structure that defines specific parameters and uses those parameters arbitrarily to discriminate against its citizens.

The state contradicts itself in several ways given these examples: (1) all citizens of the state must be autonomous and self-sufficient—yet the state defines some of its citizens as dependent; (2) citizens who are defined legally, politically, and economically as dependent, when it is of economic interest to the state, are required to act in a capacity that has not been encouraged or facilitated by the state (that is, support themselves as independent agents) when their particular circumstances alter, as in the case of welfare mothers; (3) particular citizens (women), even after achieving a modicum of success, continue to be viewed by the state as among the dependent and must give proof of their agency: *Frontiero* v. *Richardson.* Only under extraordinary pressure has the state used strict scrutiny in examining gender discrimination in its courts. Until quite recently the category "suspect classification" had not been used to test cases of gender discrimination.

Yet, the American voting public in 1982 determined that women were "better off" within the system as it was conceived and developed, that women had "too much to lose" if the ERA were ratified. Accordingly, Stetson warns that the move toward gender-neutrality that appears to be the direction of Supreme Court decisions may obscure *actual* differences between men and women. Given these arguments, what are the alternatives?

Ratification of CEDAW would offer thorough and distinct guidelines for addressing actual differences. CEDAW incorporates Hevener's analytic categories: nondiscriminatory (Article 1), corrective (Article 4), and protective (Article 11).[40] As a mixed convention, CEDAW outlines state responsibility, not simply responsibility for direct action by the state and its agents, but also for state complicity[41] in nonstate activities (familial relations, customs, religious practices, and so on.) that (a) are pervasive and enduring in effect and (b) cause harm to a specific category of person (that is, women).[42]

CEDAW's inclusion of protective measures in Article 11 is remedial. Therefore, Article 11 also stipulates that "this article shall be reviewed periodically in the light of scientific and technological knowledge and shall be revised, repealed or extended as necessary."[43] "Protective" measures often have had the effect of infantilizing women within patriarchal systems. Accordingly, the review process mandated by Article 11 is a safeguard against continued "special treatment" of women once corrective measures have been effective and/or technological advances have eliminated the actual (rather than traditionally perceived) need for such special treatment.

The final argument for ratification of CEDAW—and human rights treaties in general—is, ultimately, a universal one. The United States must, in order to (1) maintain, if not *regain,* its position in the world community and (2) enhance global cooperation, incorporate and support international agreements that establish the primacy of human rights and the human value of all people.

Chapter 3 🐝

Globalizing Concern for Women's Human Rights

Reconceiving the Terms of the Discourse

> Discrimination is most dramatically illustrated by toleration of violence against a supposedly subordinate group and acceptance of it as a cultural norm. So long as governments do nothing to stop violence against women they are, in effect, condoning such violence and thereby depriving women of their fundamental freedoms and human rights.[1]
>
> —CEDAW Meeting Statement

The overwhelming evidence of women's subordination as a global and transhistorical phenomenon is sufficient condition for supposing that it is enduring and pervasive. Despite this evidence, the forms that oppression takes in diverse cultures are dissimilar enough to limit dialogue about the definitions of oppression and its potential remedies. Is it possible to construct a coherent voice in expression of "women's" concerns? What is international about the forms of women's subordination, where "international" is the analytic category?[2]

CEDAW is critically important as an international instrument primarily because it serves to highlight attitudes and practices in the international community as a whole. Moreover, analysis of the relative status of the treaty reveals not only attitudes and practices within member states, but also the ways that those attitudes are expressed in the United Nations itself. These attitudes and resulting behaviors continue to be detrimental to women.[3] In the preamble to the treaty, CEDAW drafters note the affirmation of the equal rights and dignity of all persons found in previous human rights instruments but are "concerned, however, that despite these various instruments, discrimination against women continues to exist." The focus of the argument in the following pages is that the organizational and normative structures of international law, informed as they are by liberal democratic and patriarchal tradition, have been a major stumbling block for women who attempt to bring their concerns to the fore.[4]

Discussion in this chapter centers around structural conditions for a worldwide women's movement with CEDAW as its central theme. The first part of the chapter identifies various types of deep structural resistance to change. This broad look at structural resistance serves as an overview of national and international reluctance to recognize women's rights as human rights. Because women have been integrally involved in sustaining cultural norms, the chapter then examines the roles that women have played in their own oppression. The third part of the chapter questions the traditional denial of women's self-identification, both by the norms within their own cultures and even by early advocates of women's rights who, though well-meaning, prematurely identified women as a group without taking into consideration the ways that women, and therefore their needs, differ. The universal definitions employed by these advocates included a considerable number of women under one umbrella of oppression but, through disregard of important differences among women, these definitions limited dialogue and undermined the project.

The Problem of State Reservations

The United Nations Commission on Human Rights is always on sensitive ground when addressing human rights violations, but there is particular resistance to interfering in what is essentially the most private arena, the family.[5] Very simply, many laws cannot reach women and girls without intruding in the private sphere. Due largely to the pervasive deference to the "private" nature of the family unit and, therefore, the private nature of violations of women's rights, the Commission on the Status of Women (CSW) has remained a data-collecting organ with little authority.[6] The lesser status and authority of CSW is made evident by the relative number of substantive reservations to CEDAW when compared to other human rights documents and the relative lack of funds to investigate claims and finance meetings of CSW.

Those states willing to become party to CEDAW have entered reservations to the treaty at an unprecedented level.[7] There are two types of reservations: procedural and substantive. Procedural reservations are less destructive to the intent of the treaty in that they simply modify the manner in which the treaty is incorporated and/or enforced. Substantive reservations, on the other hand, are reservations that eliminate or substantially modify wording that is intrinsic to the nature and intent of the treaty, thus destroying the integrity of the instrument. Substantive reservations also preclude the possibility of universality in promotion and protection of women's human rights given the variability of the document as a result of the specific reservations entered by states parties to the convention.

Nevertheless, universality is a primary goal of international human rights law, and the fact that states become party to a convention is a positive first step. States parties to a convention are able to communicate more clearly among themselves about the specifics of the issue at hand. The commitment to the intent of the treaty implied by ratification and the public nature of subsequent claims encourages states to accept responsibility for activities that violate the treaty—whether those activities are carried out by the state directly or are simply culturally pervasive violations. Not unexpectedly, when reservations are entered to such an extent that they alter the fundamental nature of the treaty, the basis for communication is lost.

Attempts to ensure the ability to communicate about particular issues have had varied success. One such effort, the document that sets guidelines for ratification and adherence to a treaty, is the Optional Protocol. Yet, in what appears to have been a colossal lack of foresight, no protocol was established regarding ratification of CEDAW. Not until the Beijing Conference in 1995, was an attempt made to remedy that considerable oversight. As a result, substantive reservations had been entered prior to the conference with relative impunity. Even though states enter substantive reservations in relation to most human rights instruments, this is particularly true in the case of CEDAW. When treaties are as heavily reserved as CEDAW is, ratification does not ensure the desired universality. So, while it may be good that states do ratify a particular treaty through substantive reservation, that treaty may be rendered virtually meaningless. This dilemma is one that has confounded efforts toward universal agreement on the most effective way to handle reservations to human rights treaties.[8]

Disregard for the integrity of human rights instruments has reached a heretofore unprecedented level in the form of substantive reservations to CEDAW. Therefore, it is not surprising that the Economic and Social Council (ECOSOC)—the body within the UN system to which CSW reports—remains reluctant to address culturally sensitive issues such as women's rights. In fact, ECOSOC reluctance has reinforced the notion that reservations to this treaty are somehow more acceptable than reservations to other instruments.[9] As a result of these conditions, CSW has been severely hampered in advancing the treaty's objectives.

The high number and broad scope of reservations to CEDAW have become a matter of considerable concern to CSW.[10] Not only are the rights that the treaty sets forth viewed as derogable, in some cases the protections afforded by the instrument are virtually eliminated. The extent to which this convention has been reserved has caused women's rights advocates to refer to ratification as "club membership" with no regard for the responsibilities attached to that membership.[11]

CEDAW has come under particular attack because it represents such an encompassing effort to alter conditions that are oppressive to women.[12] The treaty offers comprehensive and broad-ranging support for women without denying their various lived experiences within each cultural milieu.[13] Yet, the treaty is viewed by many states party to the treaty as a direct threat to traditional ideas of state stability, religious practices, and the integrity of the family. As a consequence, the high number of ratifications of CEDAW (as of December 1995, 141 states had ratified the treaty) is offset by the considerable number of substantive reservations entered by states party.

Substantive reservations have two broad-ranging consequences. First, they alter the form of the convention in that certain components are eliminated entirely. Secondly, others are adjusted in order that the convention adhere to pre-existing domestic structures. Reservations of this magnitude are inherently damaging to the universality of the convention. In May 1990, Else Annette Grannes reported on the ninth session of the Committee on Elimination of Discrimination against Women. Under section 3.5 on reservations she says:

> An alarming number of States parties have not made an unconditional acceptance of the Convention [CEDAW], but have ratified or acceded subject to reservations. The most problematic category of reservations is the substantive one.[14]

Some states enter substantive reservations to such an extent that CEDAW conforms almost entirely to their pre-existing laws and customs. In other words, these states adhere to norms required by CEDAW only insofar as they would have in the absence of the convention. Yet this situation has failed to move the ECOSOC to review the status of the treaty:

> It thus becomes apparent that any attempt to address the issues included in CEDAW presents serious pressures on international human rights bodies. The issues are complicated, broad and hard to deal with. In large part for this reason, women's issues are not commonly dealt with in the mainstream international human rights debates and bodies of the UN, or by the international human rights NGOs.[15]

Because altering the status of women is inconsistent with UN member states' fundamental beliefs and conventional behaviors, efforts to broach the subject of violations with an offending state create considerable tension.[16] When ECOSOC has attempted to do so it has been faced with claims of imperialist behavior and infringement on state sovereignty. Quite understandably, ECOSOC has been extremely averse to raising these potentially divisive issues.

Resistance within ECOSOC

The specific conditions that work against ECOSOC support when CSW requests discussion of religious and cultural practices that harm women are:

1. other human rights issues are viewed by members as more critical and tension over this issue could create difficulty in negotiation on these "more critical" issues;[17]

2. few women are state representatives to mainstream committees and commissions that are not specifically mandated to address women's issues;[18]

3. there is considerable resistance to intervention in or criticism of any practice that is viewed as inherent to a given culture;[19]

4. the sanctity of the family "protects" the space in which most women find themselves in virtually all cultures, and altering that condition requires the political will to rework social as well as legal structures; and[20]

5. women face extreme uncertainty in their attempts to bring about change in their own lives therefore the voice that has been raised in protest is an understandably tentative one.[21]

This last point is doubly important because the integrity of the struggle to assert women's fundamental rights, internationally, depends upon respecting diversity among women.[22] Sustaining a "coherent voice" and collective support for the mechanisms that promote women's liberation and equality, in the face of such diversity, has been difficult at best. But only by respecting difference can there be any assurance that the issues addressed are those that women themselves find critical to their welfare. Because UN lack of support indicates member states' lack of interest, the challenge that women inevitably face is finding the ways and means to continue to assert their human rights within their own state systems while at the same time maintaining the integrity of the distinctions among and between themselves.

For example, fundamental resistance to dealing directly with violations of women's rights once they are made public by CSW must come from state representatives to the mainstream UN bodies whose function it is to determine necessary and appropriate action.[23] Given the ambivalence around—if not outright rejection of—the legitimacy of women's claims, the situation seems overwhelming. What is worse, political and cultural resistance are not the only factors that inhibit attention to women's harms. In the past, the problem was partly geographic: The physical distance between CSW and ECOSOC—CSW met in Vienna and ECOSOC is based in Geneva—made it more difficult for the two bodies to communicate. But the primary reason for CSW's isolation remains the relative lack of political will among representatives to the UN mainstream bodies to question traditional norms and to meet the challenge posed by claims of cultural relativism and Western imperialism.[24]

International Reification of Patriarchal State Structures

Patriarchy is a structural commonality across most cultures and so provides a beginning point for discussion of the United Nations as an international organization of states. The characteristics of patriarchal institutions relevant to this study include: the division of labor, the definition of family, the definition of motherhood, and a set of values concerning economic development.[25] These definitions and values have been important in virtually all cultural settings and are in that sense universal. But they cannot be universalized in any concrete way because they are as unique in application as they are comprehensive in effect. Sarah Brown makes a compelling point:

> We cannot hope to describe or explain patriarchy by identifying it solely with actors, be they men or states. As a system its structure is more than their sum. . . . there is little point on this view in looking for any "essence" of patriarchy, beyond the forms which it takes in different historical structures.[26]

This is, again, one of the confounding elements in identifying commonalities through which one might define the essence of women's oppression. How does one describe something that takes different forms given its environment, but is, in effect, if not in intensity, the same?

If issues are to be addressed with sensitivity to variations in women's situations and choices, it may be helpful to rely on what Jack Donnelly refers to as "levels of specificity,"[27] and to abstract to the "level" at which the problem may be addressed universally. So even though universal agreement is critical, real concentration on violations of women's rights must originate at the "grassroots level": the level at which violations occur and, therefore, are at least initially defined and addressed. As an instrument focused on alleviating women's oppression, CEDAW makes possible the objectivity that encompasses disparate concerns while it facilitates direct action locally. (See appendix).

Another hurdle in the struggle to define women's rights as human rights at the international level has historically been the existence of ostensibly neutral rules of law at the state level. In fact, legal structures at the state level reflect and reinforce conventional biases in which women are not acknowledged—except as they fulfill their proscribed functions.[28] Consequently, it has not been enough to recognize women as equal before the law as it exists. Laws have traditionally protected the family unit from interference by the state with the father/husband as the representative of the family in the larger society. Because that tradition has been influential in the development of international instruments,[29] the same disregard for the contributions that women make also dismisses the violation of their rights as a private matter—both nationally and internationally.[30] Alternatively, laws that, for example, identify spousal rape as a crime do not simply promote equality before the law.[31] On the contrary, laws making spousal rape a crime indicate a sensitivity to the ways that the legal structure has been indifferent to the abuses that women suffer, and are direct efforts to protect women— not simply under the law, but within the culture. One of the fundamental realities of women's lives is that they have traditionally been recognized as extensions of (as protected by) male representatives in the public arena. The state has therefore failed to afford women the agency required if they are to challenge their "protected" status.

The "protective" legislation that is endemic to patriarchal society, according to Hevener, delimits women's freedom.[32] In their efforts toward equity, women are requesting legislation that affords them basic rights. For instance, legal reform that attempts to eliminate inequities must, first, reflect sensitivity to prevailing norms of oppression and, second, be subjected to review in light of societal changes.[33] CEDAW (in section 3 of Article 11) states:

> Protective legislation relating to matters covered in this article shall be reviewed periodically in the light of scientific and technological knowledge and shall be revised, repealed or extended as necessary.[34]

Because traditions that oppress women have sustained attitudes and activities that remain unexamined in the context of contemporary society,[35] states ratifying CEDAW are expected to incorporate the notion of social change into their legal structures. However, despite ratification, states continue to see their responsibility as very limited. The transition is a difficult one to make primarily because states have not been held responsible for the conventional behavior of their citizenry. States have simply been condemned or sanctioned for their own active violations of their citizens' human rights. As a result, oppressive traditions remain unexamined in most societies.[36] CEDAW requires states to recognize women as equal before the law and, where necessary, as a result of the increased awareness of women's rights as human rights, CEDAW Article 2(f) requires states to work actively toward safeguarding women against conventionally accepted behaviors that constitute direct violations of their human rights. Unlike other human rights instruments, CEDAW does not mandate preemptive regard for protection of the family unit when that protection is a direct violation of a woman's rights or is a form of oppression,[37] but holds the state responsible for actively protecting women from those violations of their rights (Article 16). This change in perspective requires states, in many cases, to redefine what it means to be a citizen.

The following sections investigate the power of traditional state definitions of citizen and the struggle women face (1) to call into question those definitions given the ambivalence inherent in such a revolutionary departure from traditional norms; (2) to gain legitimacy for their own claims at the international level, which means universalizing their concerns (in order to be heard) without developing yet another exclusionary discourse; and, finally, (3) to find support for implementation once state ratification has occurred.

Early Efforts toward Equality

During the drafting of the Universal Declaration of Human Rights (and as a result of the insistence of representatives from the Commission on the Status of Women), it took three sessions of the Human Rights Commission before agreement was reached on alternative wording for "all men" and "like brothers" in Article 1. The more precisely applicable term "human beings" was used only after considerable struggle. "Human beings" was not even the terminology agreed upon within that third session (the majority preferred the phrase "all people, men and women"). Nonetheless, according to Johannes Morsink,[38] when the term "human beings" appeared in the final document, it was never contested—nor was it spoken of again in open session.

Some of the women present at these sessions (most notably Eleanor Roosevelt) repeatedly remarked that the use of the term "men" meant men and women "without differentiation."[39] This statement is indicative of the ambivalence—even among strong women's advocates—that has continued to prevail in international fora when dealing with violations suffered specifically by women. Given this equivocation, even among women who were deeply involved in the development of international instruments, it is reasonable to assume that strong traditions will remain compelling in the face of the uncertainty that is inherent in fundamental change.

Identifying women's issues as a specific area of international concern is also made considerably more difficult by virtue of the critical nature of women's cultural roles. Women do not usually see themselves, nor are they seen, as a separate and distinct group (for example, a social class)[40] over which active control has been maintained. The functions that they serve form an integral link between the past and the possibility of a future. Thus, continuation of the practices that oppress women is predicated upon their complicity—their active involvement in their own exploitation. Altering the conditions of women's existence requires an awareness by women of alternatives. Progress also requires access to the means of effecting change, access that may not be readily available to them as women.[41] Hilary Charlesworth says it very well:

> The structure of the international legal order reflects a male perspective and ensures its continued dominance. The primary subjects of international law are states and, increasingly, international organizations. In both states and international organizations the invisibility of women is striking. Power structures within governments are overwhelmingly masculine: women have significant positions of power in very few states, and in those where they do, their numbers are miniscule.[42]

It should not be surprising, therefore, that the attention of the international community to issues that concern women did not occur in response to women's plight.

The United Nations' direct involvement in affecting the situation of women occurred when, as a result of studies outlining the third world crises in population and food early in the 1970s, the UN system was forced to recognize the importance of women's contributions, and the critical nature of their roles, in each of those areas of life. At that time there were virtually no women in the mainstream UN system in a representative capacity. Still a far cry from sensitizing itself to the diverse voices of women and with few mechanisms by which to avail itself of their collective knowledge, the UN unanimously adopted a recommendation from CSW that 1975 be declared International Women's Year (IWY).[43] Unfortunately (though predictably), the focus within the mainstream UN system was *not* the liberation and equality of women, but the ways in which women could be instrumental in the effort to address the aforementioned crises. However, one result of the crisis in population in particular was recognition of the right to family planning. According to Hilkka Pietila and Jeanne Vickers, "With this right as a practical, everyday asset women the world over have moved into a new age: one in which they may eventually have the right to control their own lives."[44] The right to control their own bodies in this way opened up a whole realm of possibilities to women: education, development of skills, and involvement in politics. Many women's advocates were, understandably, optimistic. Only during the subsequent Decade for Women (1976–1985) did feminists come to realize the overwhelming complexity of the effort to identify "women's issues" and to get them on the international agenda.

The following section highlights the tension that exists between women from various regions and their attempts to identify their commonalities in the face of seemingly insurmountable differences. The final section offers CEDAW as a viable instrument for addressing common problems without denying women's various lived experiences.

Criticism of the Western Feminist Movement

Since the World Conference in Mexico City (1975) at the beginning of the Decade for Women, the efforts of women to support a global movement have redoubled, but the decade had a particularly inauspicious beginning. About the conference in Mexico, Pietila and Vickers say, "Even when the majority of delegates are women, delegations will express their official government line—and in how many countries does official policy take account of women's views and rights?"[45] Two dynamics appear to reinforce this behavior: that is, the tendency of the previously disenfranchised, when they are afforded a place of prominence, to elect to conform (in varying measure) to the agenda of the existing power structure. First, these inductees into the rarified circle are no longer outsiders criticizing the power elite. Whether consciously or inadvertently, in order to justify the confidence placed in them, they tend to align themselves with the "official government line"—that is, with the power elite. Second, when coming together with others in such a diverse setting, they feel more acutely their connection with their own cultures, thus somewhat unwittingly express the familiar (though possibly oppressive) attitudes and biases of their own systems. These attitudes and biases are more pronounced and consequently appear exaggerated given the diversity of the setting, which creates even more distance between "unlike" cultures.

Consequently, women's own resistance to unity obfuscated the focus of the conference. Eastern and Southern women were put off by the elitist, exclusionary, and narrowly defined discourse of Western, particularly American, middle-class feminists.[46] In the United States, ideas about how to succeed in the public arena had been epitomized by the atomistic, individualist male ideal. Therefore, in their struggle for visibility, women in the West had attempted to emulate the strategies of that dominant elite.[47] As a result of these criticisms, together with challenges (until this time only faintly heard) by women of color and lesbians in their own country, mainstream feminism in the United States underwent a long overdue self-analysis.[48] U.S. domestic complexities aside, women of the East and the South recognized different sets of needs. The right to food and the right to education were primary among those needs.

Despite this stumbling start, and as a result of subsequent world conferences that increased communication between and among countries, the expression of the concerns of women has undergone subtle though important changes.[49] Not the least of which changes have been the more nuanced interpretations of women's concerns and the increasing number of locally-organized programs for women's rights within each country.

Coming Together without Universalizing

In the struggle to promote women's human rights, denial of women's life experiences has no place. Women have refused to employ an exclusionary, hegemonic discourse. Rather they have incorporated difference in their struggle. Had they not, they would have been exchanging one oppressive rule for another. Historically, being understood within the system has meant using the marginalizing language of the dominant elite; a language written and proscribed by the dominant few. Because women were invisible in the public arena, there had been no language to express the harms that they suffer.[50] When women voiced discontent, their requests did not make sense within the existing public institutions—were, therefore, incoherent to those who were well served by maintenance of those institutions—and as a result were not heeded.[51]

A fundamental characteristic of patriarchy is centralized control, which mandates adherence to a dominant paradigm. Yet, it is important to note that the nature of patriarchy is such that it accrues to itself the richness inherent in ethnic, racial, gender, and sexual difference while, at the same time, denying the existence of the people who enrich society considerably by virtue of these diverse orientations. By the same token, patriarchal structures assume (in the fullest sense of the word) women's labor and exploit it.[52] For example, the quality of women's productive and reproductive contributions makes much of society possible. Yet, as mentioned earlier, traditional structures continue to "invisibilize" women's labor and deny women's changing responsibilities:

> The number of families in which women are sole supporters is on the increase. Such women are among the poorest people concentrated in the urban informal labour markets and they constitute large numbers of the rural unemployed and marginally employed. The assumptions underlying policies, research and legislation that confined the role of supporter or head of household to men should be identified and eliminated.[53]

Still, the emancipation of women is viewed by mainstream UN bodies as too "hot" an issue, as too destabilizing to social structures to be confronted at the international level. This attitude is so pervasive that it amounts to the virtual isolation of women's issues—even from other human rights issues. Belinda Clark notes:

> The failure to extrapolate the wider implications for treaty relations from the case of CEDAW reflects a view commonly implied, if not expressed, in speeches to ECOSOC and the General Assembly, that CEDAW is somehow separate and distinct from other multi-lateral treaties—even other UN human rights instruments.[54]

A great deal of concerted effort on the part of women has been necessary to combat this "ghettoization." But, unless women intend to develop a mono- lithic and exclusionary system akin to the one that has oppressed them for centuries, it will be necessary for them to incorporate various—sometimes seemingly incommensurable—perspectives in their efforts. How is it possi- ble to incorporate these disparate concerns within nonhegemonic[55] and nonexclusionary discourse?

The effort to empower women must truly operate from the "grassroots" level. Women must define themselves according to their own values and ob- jectives. A noted Western feminist legal theorist argues that, "for women to affirm difference, when difference means dominance, as it does with gender, means to affirm the qualities and characteristics of powerlessness."[56] I argue, rather, that it is not difference that must be eradicated but the attendant asymmetry in power arrangements. Denying difference is not the answer. The differences are not merely between men and women but also among women. Diversity is a fundamental truth in all cultural settings. It is not enough to argue that "we are women and therefore different from men." Women must argue that "we are different from men *and* from one another in very important ways that make us unique. Recognition and respect for those differences is critical to the health of our societies." In fact, recognition of difference is critical to any understanding of individuals and their rela- tionship to the state. Women must continue to affirm difference despite the traditional asymmetry in power arrangements and the gender-specific op- pression that is an integral part of maintaining that difference. They must also continue to affirm difference *because of* the traditional asymmetry in power arrangements: Emulation of certain forms of power may be margin- ally effective within traditional institutions, but will not necessarily alter those institutions or incorporate alternative life experiences into the main- stream discourse. If power finds its voice through the articulation of differ- ences it is not difference that must be eradicated. On the contrary, only in recognizing the legitimacy of those different characteristics can we appreci- ate and learn from a variety of perspectives.

Audre Lorde is particularly helpful in this regard:

> It is a particular academic arrogance to assume any discussion of feminist theory without examining our many differences, and without significant input from poor women, Black and Third World women, and lesbians. . . . [yet] to read this program is to assume that lesbian and Black women have nothing to say about existentialism, the erotic, women's culture and silence, developing feminist theory, or heterosexuality and power. . . . What does it mean when the tools of a racist patriarchy are used to examine the fruits of that same patriarchy? It means that only the most narrow perimeters of change are possible and allowable.[57]

Lorde claims that oppression and exclusion do not simply touch each of us externally or even in the same ways. Oppression and exclusion are internalized and acted out with the most insidious yet pervasive particularity. She further claims that it takes considerable effort to see oppression and marginalization because they are such an integral part of our selves, that neither is fully defined by any particular experience. Finally, and most importantly, it is not entirely the responsibility of the most oppressed and marginalized to articulate the problem and justify action to alter the conditions. Articulation and eradication of oppressive conditions requires the concerted effort of all who value social equity and human dignity.

Because the conditions of marginalization and oppression permeate our very existence, any effective remedy must also. To some extent marginalized people are seen (and have seen themselves) as beggars at the master's door pleading for crumbs of acceptance for the pitiable figures they are. On the contrary, Lorde is saying only those outside the house are able to point to the instability of the foundation. The Master and his entourage must come outside the house in order to discuss the damages in the light of a new day.[58] Feminists who continue to define the problem in terms of white, middle-class, heterosexual women must consider themselves part of that entourage. All aspects of our humanness must figure in the assessment of all aspects of our systemic construct. Because our differences are more pronounced and more clearly defined across state and cultural boundaries, respect for difference *must* set the international women's movement apart from traditional forms of organization.[59]

Again, the task is an arduous one: The capacity of the 1976–1985 Decade of Women to incorporate difference was challenged immediately. When, as early as the world conference in Mexico, women of other cultures rejected Western feminists' descriptions as inappropriate, the movement suffered a crisis of identity.[60] The questions that this crisis evoked included these: "If we are not speaking for all women, for whom do we speak? Can we speak for anyone without excluding those who do not recognize themselves in the narrative? How is it possible to come together as a collectivity in the face of our differing needs?" Nonetheless, possible resolutions to these difficulties, in the form of "strategies"[61] and "plans of action"[62] emerged slowly through communication and cooperation. CEDAW was the definitive instrument to emerge from that process.

CEDAW as a Viable Alternative

The most comprehensive of the international agreements adopted for the protection of women's human rights is CEDAW. Over the years, more than 150 countries have ratified the convention, but, as with human rights instruments in general and women's human rights instruments in particular, the circumstances surrounding those ratifications have been less than encouraging: The force and authority of the document has been undermined by the number of substantive reservations entered by states party.[63] Some women's advocates recognized dire consequences for the advancement of women's international human rights in light of three things in particular: (1) ratification of CEDAW is rendered meaningless with substantive reservations attached;[64] (2) location of CSW in Vienna rather than Geneva created a physical isolation from ECOSOC in addition to the ideological distance that already separates the two bodies;[65] and, (3) the only driving force behind the advancement of women's human rights was women themselves.

But the ghettoization of women's issues is not simply a function of the above conditions as much as it is an overriding resistance to incorporating perspectives that challenge the fundamental framework of the social organization within states. As indicated in Audre Lorde's address to the New York Institute for the Humanities,[66] equity for women is not simply a plea for entry, nor is it an isolated set of principles that apply selectively. Nancy Hartsock says it very clearly and concisely:

> At bottom, feminism is a mode of analysis, a method of approaching life and politics, a way of asking questions and searching for answers, rather than a set of political conclusions about the oppression of women.[67]

Ultimately, the question is not on which feminism we can agree, but which strategies are necessary to advance each cause. CEDAW combines the protections found in various human rights instruments that, while they mention women, do not concern themselves with the rights of women as a specific social group with issues unique to that group.

Major mainstream human rights instruments (for example, the Universal Declaration of Human Rights, the Covenant on Civil and Political

Rights and the Covenant on Economic, Social, and Cultural Rights) do, however, make statements as to the equal status of women. UDHR, in its preamble, talks about "the equal rights of men and women," and Article 3 of each of the two covenants mentioned above ensures the "equal right of men and women to the enjoyment" of the rights set forth therein. Yet, declaring all people equal is far from a guarantee of equal treatment under the law or gender-sensitive interpretations of law, much less equal treatment within a given cultural setting.

CEDAW is explicit in its eradication of gender discrimination in all its forms. The drafters of CEDAW realized that the wording, to be effective, must specifically address discrimination within traditional institutions and customary practices as well as governmental laws and procedures. In order to highlight gender-distinct laws and their inherent biases, CEDAW calls for, not simply "equality before the law," but a closer inspection of the laws themselves, Article 2(f). According to Article 2, the state must be proactive in seeking out and eliminating discriminatory biases in its laws and also in the conventional practices that violate women's rights. By the same token, there are biases that are mandated within CEDAW (Article 4).[68] These biases are not to be considered discriminatory, but should be recognized as an attempt to increase women's private status to the level already enjoyed by men and to ensure equal access and participation of women in public and political venues.

CEDAW is the only instrument that requires states to take responsibility for the elimination of conventionally accepted oppression of women without mention of the "sanctity of the family unit." Other instruments have placed the sanctity of the family, as the primary unit of society, before the rights of the individual.[69] Most women's advocates agree that strengthening the family unit, as it has existed, has had a deleterious effect on the struggle for equality between men and women. The privacy traditionally accorded the family ostensibly protects the unit, but many advocates of women's rights believe that the wording in UDHR (Article 12) and in ICCPR (Article 17) indicates the extent to which the practices and institutions that subjugate women and serve to strengthen the hold that men have on the productive and reproductive labor of women continue to dominate even in international law.[70]

As a case in point, the Declaration on Elimination of Discrimination against Women (DEDAW), when it was presented to the General Assembly, required the elimination of gender discrimination within both civil and criminal laws. Article 6 of DEDAW guaranteed equality under civil law, and Article 7 called for the repeal of "all provisions of penal codes which constitute discrimination against women." Yet, upon reviewing DEDAW in 1975, representatives were concerned that Article 6(1) might be destabilizing to the family as an institution, so the phrase, "without prejudice to the safe-guarding of the unity and the harmony of the family" was added before the wording of DEDAW could be agreed upon. The General Assembly seriously undermined the intent of DEDAW with the addition of that preemptive phrase.

Though CEDAW does not specifically discuss domestic violence, neither does it contain such modifying terminology. As a result, CEDAW is viewed as having the potential to interfere in the private sphere and, accordingly, has been subject to a greater number of substantive reservations than any other treaty—even human rights treaties. When women's advocates decry the number of substantive reservations entered to CEDAW, the question often raised is "what is to be preferred, a high number of ratifying states or strict adherence to the provisions—an adherence that may inhibit ratification by many states?" This question is often posed as though it were exhaustive of all possibilities. It is this totalizing resistance that limits the search for alternatives within each cultural setting.

Continued Structural Resistance to Change

In the several decades since the founding of the United Nations, state resistance to human rights treaties in general has been due, in large part, to the sensitive nature of the claims and the possible infringements on sovereignty and cultural differences that responding to such claims could entail.[71] Protection of women has been a particularly difficult area of human rights law in part because, despite the fact that women's contributions remain virtually invisible to economic and social structures, women and their roles are central to the construction and stability of economic and social realities within all societies. For example, in most countries, the work that a woman does in the home and in agriculture is unpaid labor that feeds her family. Yet, neither her productive nor her reproductive work has been included in analyzing the economy of her country.[72] This view of women as "outside" the operation of the economy, again, privatizes, delegitimizes, and in effect invisibilizes their considerable contributions.

Because women differ vastly in their needs, very different remedies are necessary to relieve women's suffering and to alleviate discrimination within each culture. Therefore, the attempt to address specific violations of women's rights becomes extremely complex from an international perspective. Zillah Eisenstein, for example, argues very persuasively that: "The doctrine of universal rights must be reinvented through a recognition of individual needs."[73] This presents a formidable challenge. Women's human rights advocates continue to focus on maintaining the balance between (1) addressing culture-specific practices with sensitivity, and (2) falling afoul of strict cultural relativist claims that constitute resistance to the perception of external interference in domestic affairs. Even so, claims of cultural relativism and the stability of the state have been used repeatedly in confounding the argument that human rights is an international concern.[74] It is through the efforts of nongovernmental organizations that the balance is maintained.

Depressurizing the Process

Nongovernmental organizations (NGOs) provide services as educators, technical resources, and often as arbiters in order to forestall some of the high-profile posturing that occurs once a state comes under censure or is being cajoled or pressured by other states to adhere to a set of standards. Working directly with women in their own unique situations, NGO assistance has made it possible for women to articulate their concerns more thoroughly, to sustain the belief that their concerns are legitimate, and to see their objectives come to fruition.[75]

As in any effort toward social change, the initial battles are fought to establish a legitimate voice within the system. Women's voices have been interpreted, negotiated, educated and refined by NGOs. These organizations have proven invaluable in grassroots efforts to educate both states and citizens. NGOs also identify and report human rights violations, but their primary function is to hear and respond to what women are saying they need—first to survive, then to develop. Women may not be entirely sure how their lives should change, but, for the most part, they are coming to recognize what they do *not* want: another form of oppression, another discourse of exclusion. Through grassroots efforts and with the help of NGOs, this has become a real possibility.[76]

The current transitions in Eastern European and African states serve to exemplify the problems inherent in a shift of political, social, and economic structures. Women are recognizing that liberal democracy (especially as it is coexistent with a market economy) is not the unambiguous "good" that it first may have appeared to be. Within this restructuring women are, for example, being forced to relinquish rights to employment in deference to male heads-of-households. In the face of these transitions, women are recognizing that liberalism and democracy as they have been defined within national and international fora have as their central premises an economic and social stability that privileges traditional structures—premises that liberal and even socialist feminist theories do not attempt to dispel. As a consequence, many women are refusing to embrace liberal and socialist feminist theories in their present forms, because wholesale acceptance eliminates discussion of alternative structures and denies the particularity of their situations. Thus, it is vitally important for women to continue to express their concerns and to adopt critical positions during these transitions.

Though chaotic, processes of transition offer women the opportunity to promote egalitarian practices and to establish institutions that endeavor to represent the entire populace. Women must offer alternatives that counter the assumptions and displace the institutions that posit recognition of women's human rights as undermining the stability of the state. Such institutions have authorized and perpetuated the vilification of those who advocate women's participation—those who insist that a radicalization of the concepts "liberal" and "democratic" is necessary to incorporate women in the discourse surrounding political and social transformation.[77] Despite the power of tradition, and in order to effect change, women must negate these premises.

Boundaries between the public and the private in the United States have become more porous over time, but the boundaries are, just as the metaphor suggests, filters through which women must pass. It is not surprising that women in Eastern Europe and Africa reject both liberal and socialist feminist theory in that neither of these frameworks critiques the centrality of economic factors in determining state action.

Within a market-based economy, a sound critique of the connection between economic and political concerns is imperative. The absence of such a critique serves to sustain the traditional emphasis on the marketplace in which the default actors are male. Women, if they wish to be recognized as legitimate actors, have been forced to deny disruptive, incommensurate characteristics of the self; must in fact, "leave behind"—in the private sphere—the gendered self. This necessary exclusion of women denies the state the benefit of their input and maintains the structure of oppression and marginalization that has existed over centuries. As Eisenstein clearly states, "There is something very old about theories of democracy premised on a citizenry assumed to be male, and a politics which is reduced to the relations of power within the economy and market."[78]

Conclusion

The primary focus of this chapter has been to illustrate that the reconciliation of commonality and diversity within the context of a world movement is critical to the protection of women's human rights. Women are charting new territory in their efforts to combat oppressive and marginalizing structures that have dominated their lives for centuries and to reconstitute the conditions of their lives. The struggle that women face is not simply against patriarchal institutions, structures, and traditions; the struggle is also against their own fears. Most women have never seen what they want to be;

they have never experienced the way they want to live. They are, therefore, struggling against the fear that what they are fighting for is an unrealizable fiction.

The secondary, but not less important, focus here is state ratification of CEDAW. Resistance to ratification of CEDAW without substantive reservations is multifaceted: political, economic, cultural/historical, sociological, psychological, structural, and religious. Given these conditions, it would seem that opposition to ratification is overwhelming, but changes are being made slowly and women have learned much through the services of NGOs.[79] However, specific resistances to addressing the concerns of women remain powerful, especially when efforts to protect women are posited as contrary to the interests of the state.[80]

Chapter 4 🐝

International Human Rights and American Foreign Policy

The Schizophrenic State

And what right have we, Sir, to trumpet our ideals of freedom and justice to other countries when we can shake out from our most respectable newspapers any day of the week eggs like these?[1]

—Virginia Woolf, *Three Guineas*

The United States wields a great deal of power in the international community. In fact, the political hegemony enjoyed by the United States is virtually unparalleled. Further, the United States has no rival in military force and it ranks among the most powerful economic forces in the world.[2] Economic influence, even more than military power, offers the state holding that influence considerable sway in determining the productive viability and technological development of less affluent states. Therefore, U.S. foreign aid has been a key factor in establishing and reinforcing attitudes and encouraging activities in international settings. Very simply, U.S. behavior in world politics matters.[3]

Since the end of World War II and the crisis of legitimacy represented by the ex post facto prosecution of the Nazis for war crimes, the international community has recognized its responsibility for establishing minimum standards and monitoring states' behavior toward their own citizens. The United States played a central role in the trials at Nuremberg and, subsequently, maintained a particularly influential position in the nascent global human rights community.[4] In fact, the United Nations itself was conceived of and guided in its development by members of the Western Alliance, particularly the United States. Yet, U.S. foreign and domestic policy on human rights has, since the 1940s, been less than consistent with its own rhetoric relative to the United Nations' universal promotion and protection of human rights. For example, the United States' recent denunciation of Serbian leader, Slobodan Milosevic, for war crimes sits rather uncomfortably with its opposition to the establishment of a permanent International Criminal Court. These and similar contradictions in U.S. behavior with regard to international relations and foreign policy evoke the image of a profound "disconnect"—a kind of schizophrenic split—between U.S. behaviors and its own assertions about itself. That image and those contradictions are the focus of this chapter.

The U.S. Constitution invokes ideals of human freedom and equality. The political, economic, and legal systems of the United States are based on a profound faith in liberty, which finds its origins in Enlightenment conceptions of human reason, value, and autonomy. Yet these systems are also founded upon a strong sense of the collectivity—of the common good—and an ethic of equal access. Therefore, an uneasy alliance between liberty and equality resides at the heart of liberal democracy in the United States. Consequently, despite its avowed commitment to human rights, the United States has frequently failed to demonstrate behavior consistent with those values.[5]

Not unexpectedly, this uneasy alliance between liberty and equality found expression in the creation of the major international human rights covenants. Even though the United States was nowhere near the height of its power in the mid-1940s, the propensities and contradictions of the liberal democratic system were substantially reified in early international human rights instruments and, as a result, the institutions that developed around them. The substantial disconnect between U.S. rhetoric and behavior can therefore be examined through the lens of the inherent contradiction between U.S. involvement in the development of human rights documents and its subsequent response to the major human rights treaties it had helped to create. However, before examining the ways that the international covenants reconstitute the tensions inherent in the U.S. system, it is necessary to understand the characteristics and dynamics that have operated to prevent U.S. development of a coherent human rights policy in its foreign relations.

Quite frankly, the United States has not acquitted itself well in its global responsibility. It has failed to exemplify the standards it so freely claims as its own.[6] The dynamics that have clearly affected the position of the United States on human rights in international affairs are (1) Cold War priorities and (2) the interaction of U.S. elitism and a peculiar form of isolationism. These two very distinct, yet related, historical dynamics in U.S. foreign policy are inextricably bound to U.S. attitudes and behaviors with regard to its human rights policy over the past five decades. Because the United States is the one remaining superpower and therefore wields inordinate power, these dynamics have significantly obstructed advancement of human rights as an international concern. How did these conditions arise?

During the Cold War era, bipolar tension between the "superpowers" (the United States and the former Soviet Union) forced the subordination of human rights to the more critical concerns for national security and the creation of alliances for purposes of stability. These concerns, both individually and in concert, had a detrimental, even stultifying, effect on the promotion and protection of human rights globally. Both the United States and the former Soviet Union used their economic and military power to gain the allegiance of states that depended heavily on foreign assistance. What followed was a virtual tug-of-war in which disregard for aid recipients' records on human rights prevailed. The primary interest of each superpower was to advance its respective ideology and enhance its own security. These conditions effectively eliminated the possibility of advancing, through the manipulation of aid, a consistent policy on human rights protection. In fact, the United States has supported some of the most repressive regimes in the world. David Forsythe reminds us:

> American anticommunism progressively became primarily not a moral crusade but a power struggle. And this power struggle came to outweigh competing values. For example, the United States (unlike its democratic allies) supported Greek military rule (1967–74) despite its harsh repression of democracy. Likewise, the United States supported colonial Portugal in its violent and oppressive policies in Africa.[7]

However, the following quote by Jeane Kirkpatrick illustrates that even late in the Cold War when attempts were made to incorporate human rights considerations into foreign policy decisions, there was a vast divide separating ideological perspectives on the proper use of power and influence:

> In Iran and Nicaragua the Carter administration and the State Department withheld economic aid, weapons, ammunition, and moral support and urged the departure of the Shah and Somoza because the administration had a theory that these acts would promote human rights and build democracy in those countries. It is not necessary to believe that the United States "lost" Iran and Nicaragua to understand that our policies failed to produce the expected consequences.[8]

The emphasis of Kirkpatrick's assertion is that U.S. action did not enhance U.S. power, that is, the United States "lost" the two countries to communism. Her position, and in fact that of most foreign policy advisors who came to prominence during the Cold War, is essentially "better a dictator who is friendly to the United States than a government that is communist." Forsythe, on the other hand, implies that there is a moral imperative that must be part of the analysis of any action by a liberal democratic state; that even though consideration must first be given to security, at some point one must evaluate both the internal consistency of the action and the message conveyed by the action. The Carter administration's actions in Iran and Nicaragua were consistent with U.S. rhetoric and sent the message that having a popularly supported regime in place (that is, a democracy) is key to receiving assistance from the United States. Kirkpatrick's criticism of Carter's policy highlights the perceived need to ensure U.S. access to the power elite in those countries, and to impose an order that is comfortable for the United States rather than allowing the countries' internal dynamics to govern their development.

As in most situations, the lens through which events are viewed determines the interpretation. Had the United States had a coherent human rights policy in place—one that was institutionalized and supported by Congress and the American people—the events noted by Kirkpatrick might have been interpreted quite differently. Further, there may have been a concerted effort to maintain a relationship with each country throughout their transitions. At that time, however, most of foreign policy was still carried out in an atmosphere of skepticism. The prominence afforded security issues was inevitable early in the Cold War era given the efforts of the United States to establish itself as a world power and its resistance to the very real threat of the Soviet rise to power and dominance in the world. However, one wonders why, in the waning years of the Cold War, people like Kirkpatrick were still concerned more with resistance to the spread of communism than with encouraging developing countries to democratize relatively autonomously, that is, with U.S. support but without undue U.S. influence. This is especially perplexing when, as early as 1962, the argument was being made quite convincingly that democratization was the key issue in the stabilization of international relationships.[9]

As important as the priorities of the Cold War years were in shaping the attitudes surrounding American foreign policy, they also served to obscure other operative dynamics. U.S. foreign policy decisions were not simply necessary and appropriate reactions to a real or perceived threat of the spread of communist and totalitarian regimes. How then does one explain the continued refusal to emphasize human rights protections in U.S. foreign policy? The increasing internationalization of corporate interests is one possibility. Regarding the use of export-import loans, Forsythe notes:

It is not surprising that Ex-Im loans ceased to be even a limited tool for the attempted protection of human rights during the Reagan administration. In an era of U.S. trade imbalances and growing concern about the U.S. ability to compete successfully in world markets, there was little inclination in Washington to restrict U.S. exports in the name of human rights. Indeed, in Congressional hearings on the Ex-Im Bank during the first Reagan administration, human rights was a subject of no consequence whatsoever.[10]

Clearly, the continued fear of communism in the United States had more to do with the expansion of markets and cultivating of resources that with moral and ideological concerns. As a matter of fact, George Soros claims:

> The open societies of the world—commonly referred to as the West— exhibited considerable cohesion in the face of the enemy. But after the collapse of the Soviet system, open society, with its emphasis on freedom, democracy, and the rule of law, lost much of its appeal as an organizing principle and global capitalism emerged triumphant.[11]

Nonetheless, in the wake of the dissolution of the Soviet Union and in light of the restructuring and democratization that is occurring in much of Eastern Europe, Asia, and Africa in the past decade, a real potential for change in the world exists. Reduction in bipolar tension and the willingness of states to incorporate democratic ideals has offered a window of opportunity—that is, the political space—to remedy conditions of oppression. Yet, the United States has not availed itself of the opportunity to rethink its foreign policy. Nor has it engaged in serious, sustained debate over its own incorporation of human rights instruments. On the contrary, the United States has become increasingly conservative over the last decade. For example, following Gorbechev's appointment and his institution of perestroika in the Soviet Union in 1989, one could not continue to explain U.S. behavior on human rights through reference to past threats. Yet, the United States has not been proactive in ratifying and incorporating human rights instruments, nor has it taken the lead in advancing human rights as a core issue in international affairs. Current U.S. subordination of human rights concerns to security and economic interests with regard to China is a further indication of the legitimacy of Soros' claim. In effect, the United States is failing in its self-assigned role because of two very distinct and intransigent characteristics— elitism and isolationism. But, what exactly do these terms mean with regard to U.S. attitudes and behaviors?

The view that the United States holds of itself as exempt from ratification and incorporation of the very treaties that it helped to create exacerbates the belief in U.S. elitism that is already pervasive in the world community. The refusal to ratify human rights treaties and to incorporate their measures in domestic law is essentially a refusal to offer itself up to the scrutiny of other states parties. U.S. elitism also dictates that the United States will not be party to treaties ratified by those "thugs" who do not intend to live up to their agreements. In fact, rather than develop a more thorough understanding of the issues through national public debate with the intention of authorizing and serving to reinforce human rights treaties globally through its own accession and ratification, the United States points to violations by other states and decries the sad state of international agreements. Diane Orentlicher wrote in 1992:

> Advances have occurred most conspicuously in the realm of bilateral policy, leaving the United States open to charges of arrogance and hypocrisy for promoting other states' compliance with internationally recognized human rights while declining to ratify major human rights treaties itself.[12]

These views and behaviors of the United States are rather easily demonstrated and are, for the most part, undisputed. The other assertion—that of U.S. isolationism—is less easily illustrated.

Earlier in the chapter, I referred to U.S. isolationism as of a "peculiar" nature—as a deviation from the traditionally understood definition of the term. That the United States has, and is, engaged both economically and militarily with the rest of the world is not in question. The relevant question is the openness of public discourse in the United States around international issues, what form the discourse takes and how the dissemination of information might tend toward the type of isolationism to which I refer. The peculiar nature of U.S. isolationism is best described by Michael Clough of the Stanley Foundation when he explains why there is an "absence of serious debate among foreign policy elites over the need to dismantle policymaking structures put in place to fight an enemy that no longer exists." I summarize the points here, but recommend a more thorough reading. Why lack of change? According to Clough, the answer is threefold:

> First, most of the principal protagonists in the debate over reshaping foreign and defense policy institutions are beneficiaries of the existing system [. . .] Second, the foreign policy community, old and new, is confused and uncertain about the nature of national interests and the role that the United States should play in the world [. . .] Third, *most members of the foreign policy community remain deeply skeptical about public involvement in the foreign policy process.* [emphasis mine][13]

No, the United States has not been isolationist in the traditional sense. The United States has been active, economically and militarily, in the global community. However, the "ever-widening chasm" between the policy elites and the American public virtually assures lack of support for an "activist global policy." A public that remains uninformed and disconnected tends to be skeptical about the benefits of, for example, the North Atlantic Free Trade Agreement (NAFTA) and is in fact isolationist with regard to foreign policy. In the absence of queries from an informed public, policymakers (including the media) enjoy unrestrained power in setting a policy that, as a result of the uncertainty identified by Clough, is necessarily—at least economically—protectionist. According to Soros, democracy and capitalism are necessary components of an open society. Yet, we go too far when we allow a global market to act as a substitute for a global society, when the poor nations of the world are used as sources of raw material and cheap labor rather than en-couraged and supported in their development:

> As long as capitalism remains triumphant, the pursuit of money overrides all other social considerations. Economic and political arrangements are out of kilter. The development of a global economy has not been matched by the de-velopment of a global society. The basic unit for political and social life re-mains the nation-state. The relationship between center and periphery is also profoundly unequal. If and when the global economy falters, political pres-sures are liable to tear it apart.[14]

The International Covenant on Economic, Social, and Cultural Rights (ICESCR) is problematic from the perspective of capitalism because it raises global redistributive issues. ICESCR also emphasizes the need for a global society rather than an expanded global market.

> The popular inclination in the United States is to go it alone, but that would deprive the world of the leadership it so badly needs. Isolationism could be justified only if the market fundamentalists were right and the global econ-omy could sustain itself without a global society . . . With the right sense of leadership and clarity of purpose, the United States and other like-minded countries could begin to create a global open society that could help to stabi-lize the global economic system and to extend and uphold universal values. The opportunity is waiting to be grasped.[15]

Yet, liberals and conservatives alike are alarmed by talk of redistribution. When coupled with historic resistance to opening foreign policy decisions to public debate, the issue becomes prohibitively controversial. Given the be-havior of the United States with regard to human rights treaty ratification and its failure to promote human rights in its foreign policy, one could as-sume that all treaties are viewed by the United States as unnecessary, even su-perfluous, in terms of U.S. adherence. This is not the case. In fact, the

United States has ratified the International Covenant on Civil and Political Rights (ICCPR), among others. The question then becomes each treaty's relationship to the U.S. system; the extent to which each conflicts with or reifies the U.S. system. Each relationship constitutes a complicated set of connections. The following section clarifies the relationship and tensions between the two covenants, connects those tensions to the systems from which the treaties emerged, and, finally, identifies the limitations of each with regard to the protection of women.

The International Bill of Human Rights: Laudable Yet Limited

The International Bill of Human Rights comprises three documents: The Universal Declaration of Human Rights (UDHR), the International Covenant on Civil and Political Rights (ICCPR), and the International Covenant on Economic, Social and Cultural Rights (ICESCR). UDHR is the document that sets forth the aspirations of the states that created the United Nations in 1945. Yet, as a purely aspirational document, UDHR does not require ratification and is not binding on signatories. Because real commitment to these goals was of the utmost importance, the United Nations spent two decades developing treaties that would give substance to these aspirations. It offered ICCPR and ICESCR for signature and ratification in 1966. These two treaties, unlike UDHR, are binding upon the state once ratified.

Protections provided by ICCPR are virtually identical to the aspirations of the ideal liberal democratic state. ICCPR emphasizes the protection of citizens' negative rights against government interference in private affairs and provides the most fundamental of the human rights protections, that is, against torture, slavery, and arbitrary detention. Yet, even ICCPR was not ratified by the United States until 1993. Its sister instrument, ICESCR, is still suspect in the West. It was particularly so before the end of the Cold War, because the covenant proposed that government legitimacy has to do primarily with state economic intervention and provision of citizens' fundamental needs. For example, ICESCR provides positive rights such as rights to food, employment with circumscribed work hours, and group rights to self-determination.

These rights are not a priority for states in the industrialized North and West because they continue to believe that a free market will ultimately ensure equity. But, to the newly forming socialist democratic states in Africa and Asia, which focus more on collective or group rights than on individualist conceptions of the good, the state must be responsible for providing the basic necessities. Therefore, the provisions under ICESCR are deemed more critical to their welfare. Each of the covenants does, however, reify the public/private dichotomy inherent to the liberal state that has traditionally served to exclude women. The following three viewpoints, thus, come into significant conflict. Liberal democratic states believe that ICCPR is fundamental, but that ICESCR is unworkable and ultimately economically destructive. Newly established socialist democracies claim that ICESCR is indispensable and that the protections provided by ICCPR must remain secondary. Women of all regimes and geopolitical locations recognize that insofar as the treaties sustain and reinforce traditional structures and institutions that exclude women, the protections they provide are inadequate in the absence of the International Convention on the Elimination of All Forms of Discrimination against Women (CEDAW).

The public/private dichotomy that invisibilizes women is inherent to the liberal democratic system and is unquestionably reinstituted in ICCPR. The limitation of ICESCR is that even though it provides positive rights to food and employment that are unavailable under ICCPR, it nevertheless assumes the same public sphere within which women are invisable. For example, ICESCR provides rights to cultural expression, yet, the group being protected from interference may oppress its women. Maintaining cultural patterns and connections through mandating group rights to self-determination could, in that case, serve to perpetuate that oppression.[16] On this account, neither ICCPR nor ICESCR extend protection to women. Hence, the argument that CEDAW is a necessary augmentation to IBHR. However, the alternative argument—the one that blocks ratification in the United States—that ICESCR goes too far has two proponents.

ICESCR does not "sit" well with at least two factions in disputes over U.S. ratification. On the one hand, the end of the Cold War did not allay Western economic conservatives' fears about the more "socialist" tendencies of the treaty. On the other, strong individualist liberals argue that state intervention in private matters is a "slippery slope" toward paternalism and, ultimately, the denial of fundamental freedoms. These fears raise questions about just what the legitimate responsibility of the state is and if, in fact, that responsibility has changed with the end of bipolar tensions and the relative availability of resources.[17] At least two questions present themselves. Can the United States accept the claims of ICESCR within its own system? What does an expanded definition of state responsibility mean with regard to women and ratification of CEDAW? Setting aside, for the moment, the question of women, let us examine some of the ways that the liberal democratic state may be expanded by ratification of ICESCR.

Affording groups and certain categories of people legitimacy within the state has required even liberal democratic states to recognize and address systemically created distinctions among their citizenry. Dealing with these issues means challenging the traditional norms that tended to exclude those groups. Consequently, in its assertion that fundamental human rights are "positive" rights to such things as food and employment, ICESCR stands as a challenge to the traditional Western understanding of state responsibility. This challenge itself makes ratification unlikely, if not impossible. Because ICCPR defines the fundamental rights of human beings as civil and political and protects against *states'* "gross" violations of those rights, it is not surprising that the United States has ratified ICCPR and has not yet ratified ICESCR.

A further concern is the effect that ICESCR could have on global relationships. If we are, as Soros claims, abandoning the ideal of open society for the pragmatic operation of a global market, ICESCR would indeed be an ill fit. If, on the other hand, this period in world history is bringing us to a realization of our common humanity and the relative availability of resources, our course becomes clear. MacPherson has this to say about where we go from here if we are to make positive progress:

> Moralists and theologians have been saying for a long time that we have got our values all wrong, in putting acquisition ahead of spiritual values. This has not cut much ice in the last three or four centuries because it was inconsistent with the search for individual and national power to which market societies have been committed. But if I am right in saying that national power from now on is going to depend on moral advantage, on moral stature, then the claims of morality and power will coincide. The way to national power will be the recognition and promotion of equal human rights. And the pursuit of these ends will bring an enlargement of individual power as well, not the powers of individuals over others or at the expense of others, but their powers to realize and enjoy their fullest human capacities.[18]

The redefinition of global relationships over the last decade makes necessary a thorough reassessment of American foreign policy goals, but there is considerable confusion about how the United States sees itself changing in relation to the rest of the world. The preference of policymakers seems to be to rely on what has worked:

> Most members of the traditional foreign policy community believe there is no reason for radical changes in foreign and defense policy-making institutions. They are not convinced the system is breaking down. "We did win the Cold War after all" they point out. "We are still the most powerful country in the world! And the world is still a dangerous place. We may not need as large a standing military force as we've maintained in the past, but we've still got to worry about nuclear proliferation, terrorism and the like." In addition, many

of those in this group deny that the excesses of the national security state were all that bad. In fact, most of them would reject that descriptive term entirely.[19]

Having "won" seems a vindication of all "necessary" excesses. That vindication, coupled with the dissolution of the Soviet Bloc, also applies pressure to "hold the line." Yet, in this period of uncertainty and instability, NGOs are advancing the proposition that changes in the definitions of state responsibility and global relationships are inevitable.[20] Nonetheless, U.S. foreign policy decision-makers remain confused about what the U.S. role will be, so they are understandably conservative in their attempts to alter policy.

President Carter submitted four human rights treaties to Congress in 1977.[21] ICCPR was ratified by the United States in January of 1992. CEDAW was submitted by Carter in 1980.[22] In 1994, the Clinton administration renewed the effort to gain the advice and consent of Congress on ratification of both ICESCR and CEDAW. Early in his adminstration, President Clinton appointed Arvonne Fraser U.S. State Department ambassador to the UN Commission on the Status of Women. There had been several subcommittee hearings on the issue of women's international human rights in the years just prior to the convening of the 104th Congress in 1995 (see chapter 3). All these events seemed to indicate a positive move in terms of the incorporation of international human rights treaties. Yet, in the years following the convening of the 104th Congress, there have been virtually no hearings on human rights issues having to do with CEDAW. CEDAW is no longer on the agenda and Arvonne Fraser has since vacated her position: The United States "lost" its seat on the commission, because nonratifying states have only a limited, nonvoting role in commission proceedings.[23]

Apathy in relation to these issues, though problematic, is one thing. Yet another, more frightening, response to the question of U.S. responsibility in the world community is that voiced by the current chair of the Senate Foreign Relations Committee, Senator Jesse Helms. Helms said, in response to a question posed by John McLaughlin on "One-on-One" (a syndicated news program), that U.S. foreign aid should be limited to military aid, and military aid should be limited to regions in which the United States has an economic interest. The fact that Helms is chair of the Senate Foreign Relations Committee, in itself, illustrates a shift toward greater conservatism and isolationism within Congress.[24] The neoconservatives of the 104th Congress are focusing on reining in the "big government"/"Great Society" spending of the more liberal Congresses of the past fifty years while sustaining the idea that a failure to finance the military would result, not only in a loss of military power by the United States, but would endanger the fragile constructions of peace agreements that exist worldwide.

Tensions usually exist between the executive and legislative branches but, if Clinton's behavior in Iraq, Yugoslavia, the Sudan, Afghanistan, and Kosovo are any indication, this administration has forsaken attempts to advocate human rights in favor of "surgically" striking offending states. The combination of moral righteousness and military might liberally peppered with regret at the necessity for violence that the new-style leaders—that is, Bill Clinton, Tony Blair, and Gerhart Schroeder—evince is disturbing. They are claiming a "third way" of doing war.[25] The continuing elitism and isolationism of the United States in international affairs—and the resulting ambivalence of the United States on international human rights issues—provide a strong contextual contrast of values from which to investigate women's human rights both in the United States and abroad.

Before proceeding, however, it is necessary to clarify. At no point do I claim that U.S. ratification of either major human rights instrument is unnecessary. On the contrary, I see ratification of ICCPR and ICESCR as essential to the effective protection of human rights. Ratification of both treaties provides, at the very least, a common language among states parties. Even though ICCPR substantially reifies the liberal democratic structure in the United States, its ratification was and is an important reaffirmation of U.S. commitment to human rights. Ratification of ICESCR is critical for at least two additional reasons: (1) because this covenant raises positive rights issues, ratification could engender self-reflection in the United States with regard to international human rights and its own domestic policies (for example, ICESCR could provide a framework for overhauling an ineffective U.S. social welfare system), and (2) ICESCR's incorporation in the U.S. system is a natural precursor to ratification of CEDAW. CEDAW is not an alternative to either of the two major treaties. The interpretations of human rights by the major treaties are simply incomplete without CEDAW. Ultimately, incorporation of fundamental human rights treaties is a necessary—yet not sufficient—condition for protection of women's human rights. That said, it is important to restate my position. The protections offered by ICCPR and ICESCR do not penetrate the cultural and systemic boundaries that invisibilize women. CEDAW does.[26] Yet, the fundamental premises of mainstream human rights treaties and their effect on women have not been the subject of meaningful public debate within the United States. The absence of such debate has inhibited organizations and individuals concerned with the promotion and protection of human rights from engaging in critical discourse about our traditional understanding of universality and human rights.[27] In fact,

> The supreme challenge of our time is to establish a set of fundamental values that applies to a largely transactional, global society. Fundamental prin-

ciples have been traditionally derived from some external authority such as religion or science. But at the present moment in history, no external authority remains undisputed. The only possible source is internal. A firm foundation on which we can build our principles is the recognition of our own fallibility. Fallibility is a universal human condition; therefore it is applicable to a global society.[28]

Thus far we can see that the question of women's rights as human rights in the United States is situated within and affected by several conditions. First, and most comprehensive, is the U.S. failure to base its foreign policy decisions on a coherent program designed to promote international human rights standards. Second, is the U.S. failure to ratify, in a timely manner, major international human rights instruments. Both behaviors continue despite U.S. involvement in the creation of human rights treaties and its avowed commitment to the spirit of the instruments.[29] Third, there has been no significant public debate in the United States around the efficacy of incorporating human rights standards, much less debate over the failure of mainstream human rights documents to recognize women's rights as human rights. This final condition is a direct consequence of the two preceding behaviors. To the extent that the United States has limited its own involvement in the international debate around human rights protections, meaningful debate in the United States on esoteric issues is rendered difficult if not impossible. While these conditions exist, women's human rights will remain an "esoteric" issue at virtually all levels of human interaction.

Women's Rights:
The "Other" Dimension in International Fora

The years immediately following World War II reflected a significant change in the global attitude concerning the proper subject of international law. Until that time, state sovereignty had been recognized as virtually inviolable. Human rights law provided a challenge to that assumption: Individuals and groups now had access to the international legal system under which they had previously been invisible.

During that same period, women's rights activists in the United States continued to challenge the state legal system under which they too had been invisible. Yet, any idea that women's rights were to be protected through recourse to human rights treaties was mistaken. The relationship of women to international protections, in the form of mainstream human rights treaties, can best be represented as a hierarchical set of displacements. The fundamental mainstream human rights treaties have done little to affect the "private" conditions under which women live.

Hilary Charlesworth, for example, examines the efficacy of the three "generations" of rights from a gendered perspective and finds each wanting:

> Like national legal systems, international law is constructed within a "public" world, although national and international public spheres are often differently defined. International law operates in the most public of public worlds, that of nation states. Thus the United Nations Charter makes the (public) province of international law distinct from the (private) sphere of domestic jurisdiction; the acquisition of statehood or international personality confers "public" status on an entity, for example, for jurisdiction, representation and ownership; the law of state responsibility sorts out (public) actions for which the state is accountable from those "private" ones for which it does not have to answer internationally.[30]

In response to this enduring distinction, Celina Romany makes the argument that a state should in fact be implicated in the pervasive and enduring mistreatment of its citizens by other than its own public agents. She describes the situation of women under domestic law as existence within a "parallel state"; and as aliens within their states:

> [Romany's essay] condemns such a framework for not making the state accountable even for those violations that are the result of a systemic failure on the part of the state to institute the political and legal protection necessary to ensure the basic rights of life, integrity, and dignity of women.[31]

Consequently, in the effort to examine and understand the implications of the position of women within U.S. law, it is helpful to look at the construction of state law and that of international law separately. Yet, when each is viewed in juxtaposition to the other, an interesting parallel is revealed. The position that human beings have occupied within traditional international law is roughly equal to the position women have occupied under state law.

Traditional international law had as its proper subject states, just as traditional U.S. domestic law recognized the rights of the franchised male. Each legal system was limited to addressing the concerns before it: In the international arena, treaties and agreements addressed only relations between and among states with a strong ethic against intrusion in state domestic policy and practice; in U.S. domestic law, concern centered around the public relationships and contracts of franchised males with a strong ethic against intrusion in what was considered inherently private. Thus, the two represent very similar constructs. Simply stated, the ethic against violation of state sovereignty in international law is very similar to the ethic against intrusion in the "domestic sphere" in state law.

In traditional international law, the invisible component is the individual citizen; in state law, women are publicly invisible and exist only in the private realm of the society. Just as the only legitimate representation or protection for citizens within the international arena was the state; the only legitimate rights for human beings who existed solely within the private realm of civil society were expressed by the representative male within the "public" discourse.

The parallel in national and international structures is simply an interesting notion until one acknowledges the hierarchical nature of the two. Human rights law poses a direct challenge to the first barrier created by the definition of "subject," which, in the international arena, is the state. But if human rights law enters and affects only the public space within the state, as in the case of the two covenants, it fails to reach the location of women's harms. Again, women, their contributions, and the violations of their rights are invisibilized. For example, even if women are "gainfully" employed, the injunction in ICESCR Article 7, "equal pay for equal work," does not recognize that men are not generally employed in positions designated as "women's work" so even equality in pay remains a debatable issue.

Given the invisibility of women in state legal systems, one now recognizes that women are in the particularly unenviable position of being "twice removed" from the protections provided by mainstream international instruments. Despite the fact that the extralegal nature of human rights treaties constitutes a compromise of state sovereignty—even representing, for some, an undesirable violation of the traditional ethic of nonintervention—international human rights law still does not address conditions and issues around pervasive, yet private, harms to women. These harms are considered beyond the purview of the state, so are even more clearly beyond the auspices of international bodies.

A further complication for women is that women's harms, even when exposed for examination under mainstream human rights law, are not directly remedied by those laws. They must fit an uneasy formulaic model, as in Romany's interpretation of *Valesquez Rodriguez* v. *Honduras,* 1989.[32] In relying on cases like *Rodriguez,* which was tried by the Inter-American Court of Justice, strides may be taken to protect women, because *Rodriguez* set a precedent in which states could be said to be complicit in acts against a particular segment of the society if the violations were "pervasive" and "particular to a certain group." The central argument was that the state did not use due diligence in prosecution and thereby created a "climate in which such violations could occur." But relying on such case law does little to establish the legitimacy of women's human rights in and of itself. Reliance upon (arguably) similar cases tends to blur the distinctions that must be made between harms to women and harms generally. Women are made to "fit" within the definitions assigned to men without regard for their differences in location within each state system.[33]

It is at precisely this point that the situation for women becomes more distressing than first imagined. Very simply, if international human rights standards equal international human rights for full citizens of each state, yet women do not qualify as citizens, then protection accorded through reference to international human rights standards is not the equivalent of protection of women's human rights, hence the claim that women are "twice removed" from international protections. In an ideal world, women's rights would be included in the protections provided by one of the above "generations." Since that is not the case, the logical response to their exclusion is universal, substantively unreserved ratification of CEDAW. This is not to say that unreserved ratification of CEDAW by all states would end women's oppression. However, universal ratification without substantive reservations could (1) establish an international dialogue in which women's human rights are present, (2) enhance the process wherein NGO implementation occurs, and (3) encourage a renewed focus by international financial institutions and corporations on women as participants in development rather than simply resources to be utilized for predetermined ends.

All the above conditions serve to underscore the limitations of the liberal democratic system as a vehicle for universalizing concern for women's human rights. Mainstream human rights instruments, which have their origins in liberal democratic Western political thought, quite naturally reify some of its inherent limitations. In other words, the question is not whether incorporation of major human rights treaties would significantly alter the U.S. system. On the contrary, the premises of ICCPR accord all too well with the U.S. system and the bases of ICESCR provide only those assurances that would be available in a strong welfare state, while doing little to extend protections to women. Ultimately, the U.S. system and the international treaties that protect human rights must be subjected to the same gendered analysis. Zillah Eisenstein[34] argues that a gendered analysis would inevitably illustrate the failures of the U.S. system and the inadvisability of unreflexive acceptance of its claim that—at least with regard to its fundamental systemic structure—it exemplifies human rights. Even putting aside women's concerns, any liberal democracy modeled after the U.S. system would warrant considerable scrutiny. In fact, David Forsythe notes:

> In some circles of U.S. society, it is provocative enough to suggest that international standards on human rights could teach the United States something important on traditional foreign policy subjects pertaining to containment of adversaries, maintenance of reliable allies, and promoting economic development with dignity. But could it be that those international standards might ac-

tually teach the United States something important about itself? That, too, may fairly be considered a foreign policy issue, or at least an intermestic [sic] one.[35]

The following section provides a historical illustration of this lack of self-reflection in U.S. domestic and foreign policies over the years since the end of World War II and the resulting emergence of NGOs as a political force.

The Importance of NGOs: The Cold War Years

During the Cold War, both the United States and the Soviet Union repeatedly cited the other's perceived and real manipulation of the United Nations' agenda in order to discredit the other and to bolster their relative power and prestige in the international community. Richard Falk argues that during the Cold War years these political variables, rather than cultural entrenchment, explained resistance to treaties that were generally perceived as limits to sovereignty.[36] U.S. foreign policy was set in a highly visible and, thus, highly politicized environment during that era. Regimes that allied themselves with the United States were granted support without regard to the human rights records of those regimes: Human rights protections were quite accurately perceived by these regimes to be of little importance in their relationship with the United States.

As a consequence of U.S. behavior, the UN appeared (particularly to the Soviet Union) to be a tool of the West with which to humiliate communist countries in the global community (for example, in 1954 all named human rights abuses occurred in Eastern European/Communist Bloc countries). And, in fact, between 1945 and 1975, "the United States government manipulated the terminology of human rights to justify anti-Communist sentiment."[37] In an effort to reduce regional and ideological tensions, the UN was forced to create "themes" around human rights abuses. Development of themes served to highlight specific abuses (wherever found) rather than focusing on the behavior of a particular state or region. Yet, the United States and the Soviet Union continued to manipulate the UN politically, which greatly hindered UN efforts to gain legitimacy in the international community and to promote, in this early period of its existence, concern for human rights.

At long last, in 1978 Amendment 502B of the (U.S.) Foreign Assistance Act[38] required that no country involved in a consistent pattern of gross violations of human rights could receive assistance. But this surprisingly strong statement was modified significantly by the Harkin Amendment, which stated "unless such assistance will benefit the needy people of the countries." How such a possibility could be determined and just which institutions were required to ensure that the "needy people of the countries" actually received the aid was not included as part of the amendment. Again, commitment to actual human rights protections was halfhearted at best. During the Reagan administration, the executive and legislative branches of the U.S. government consistently failed to promote the U.S. avowed purpose:

> No security assistance was cut, much less terminated, by the Reagan adminis- tration for human rights reasons during the 1981–1984 period. Indeed, secu- rity assistance was up some 300 percent by 1984, compared to 1980.[39]

Within this breach, NGO's and grassroots organizations, which had already begun forming, took on increasingly important roles.

NGOs: Neolevelers-at-Large

Until the late 1960s when the covenants were offered for ratification, the work of the UN was not taken very seriously because of the lack of "teeth" in UDHR. Clearly, the UN had no real power. Unless states committed themselves to the protection of human rights through treaty ratification, UN influence would remain minimal. Therefore, the Commission on Human Rights continued the tedious work of development and codification of the instruments that were ultimately to be recognized as the basis for in- ternational regimes on human rights. At the same time, the number and specificity of NGOs continued to increase throughout the world. Their mo- tivation was clear: In a world where even the most liberal of governments had agendas that were not necessarily conducive to human rights promo- tion, much less protection, popular action was the only answer. As an indi- cation of the challenge that NGO's faced, Laurie Wiseberg cites three examples of U.S. behavior that, if altered, could significantly affect attitudes and sustain support for protection of human rights:[40]

1. no other nation is more heavily involved in arming and training the rest of the world militarily than the United States;
2. the United States plays a preponderant role both in bilateral and mul- tilateral economic assistance programs (billions of dollars go to highly repressive regimes: South Korea, Chile, Indonesia, the Philippines and South Africa);
3. a wide variety of federal programs support and encourage U.S. multi- national corporations, especially the major commercial banks in their "private" activities in the highly repressive nations of the world.

Why is this the case if, as it claims, the United States to embodied, from its founding, the values surrounding human rights? Even more perplexing is that, for reasons having to do with U.S. behavior, human rights organizations of the world were (and are) severely hampered in encouraging (unwilling) change within any offending state.

As a response to the atrocities committed in Vietnam and Chile and the cruelty of apartheid in South Africa, the number and diversity of NGOs increased rapidly in the 1970s. No longer was the world community using terminology like "unprecedented crimes against humanity" to describe "isolated situations."[41] Atrocities were happening everywhere around the globe. There was wide-spread agreement in nongovernmental circles that something must be done to ensure the rights of human beings worldwide. If this was not a high priority among those in power, it was at the grassroots level in many societies. Concern that fundamental freedoms and civil liberties were being abrogated with relative impunity also sparked academics to recognize the interconnectedness of the countries and peoples of the world. At the same time, technological advances were making it possible for the public to view the carnage and waste of war personally. As a result, human rights came to be viewed less as a philosophical and theoretical issue and more as a fundamental requirement for existence, the denial of which threatened the well-being of us all.

However, even in the wake of increased global commitment to human rights, women's human rights have remained an isolated issue, supported and expanded almost exclusively by nongovernmental and grassroots organizations. Very simply, accession to and unreserved ratification of fundamental mainstream human rights treaties by each state constitute great strides toward recognizing the overwhelming range of resistances to the idea that women's rights are human rights. Nonetheless, women's rights remain outside the realm of critical and necessary protections. Nongovernmental and women's grassroots organizations have done considerable work in laying the foundations and creating the institutions that make possible the incorporation of women's human rights into state and international structures. The welfare of the world's women has improved greatly through their efforts. But, U.S. ratification of CEDAW would constitute a strong reassertion of the fundamental tenets upon which the United States is founded and ratification would also serve to underscore, in the world community, U.S. commitment to human rights. Finally, U.S. ratification would constitute a reaffirmation of women as full citizens and would clearly indicate that preparation for meeting the challenge of effective institutionalization of women's rights is a state responsibility.

Expansion of NGO Influence:
Bridging the Gaps

Amnesty International (AI) was founded in 1961, it was one of a very few internationally established organizations that focused on protection of human rights. AI accepted as its mandate the "first generation" rights established in UDHR. It was not until five years later that the binding document—the International Covenant on Civil and Political Rights (ICCPR)—entered into force. By that time, the work of AI had served to reduce, significantly, East/West tensions around issues of unjust imprisonment and torture. At the very least, AI had avoided exacerbating the tensions. AI tried to depoliticize East/West animosity by targeting political imprisonment—"prisoners of conscience." Rather than point to one or the other of the powers or their respective allies, AI found the violations. AI recognized that in its efforts it must downplay the geopolitical location of the violation and focus on the violation itself. When possible, AI worked on behalf of three victims simultaneously: communist, anticommunist, and nonaligned in order to avoid the appearance of "pointing the finger" in any one direction. AI evolved as an organization whose mandate was defined through its work: The term "prisoner of conscience" was first used in 1961 and included those who suffered imprisonment as a result of (1) civil disobedience or (2) conscientious objection.[42] The process of emphasizing the conditions surrounding the alleged abuse wherever it occurred and not focusing on specific violating states came to be recognized as a useful mode of operation for human rights organizations and subsequently developed into what have been termed "regimes."[43] Because regimes focus on the violation and not on the violating state, the process was rendered less politically volatile.

Another positive result of state ambivalence in the protection of human rights was the growing interest and concern of organizations that were otherwise mandated; groups that traditionally had not seen fit to involve themselves in the international struggle. For example, churches have been instrumental in much of the work being done, and scientists have involved themselves in "investigating" abuses.[44] In recent years, AI has expanded the scope of its protections, but more encouraging is the fact that the number and specificity of NGOs increased also. As the diversity and specificity of concerned groups increased "themes" began to emerge. These themes resulted in the creation of treaties that were very specific in nature. In fact,

> [t]he "thematic mechanisms" capitalise on the UN's legitimacy as the premiere global international institution and its ability to reach out or into virtually every society, and to establish universally applicable norms. . . . [further] the mechanisms rely almost exclusively upon NGO information.[45]

Emergence of Themes: Filling the Gaps

During the first 20 years of its existence, the UN focused almost entirely on development and codification of human rights instruments. Relatively little was done to "promote" (much less protect) human rights in a proactive manner. Then, in 1966, ICCPR was offered for signature as a binding instrument that would put into practice the sentiments of Articles 2 through 21 of UDHR. The protections that ICCPR provided can be compared to advantage with nineteenth-century liberal political thought. These protections were designated the "first generation rights." ICCPR maintains that human rights are inherent to the individual and are held independent of the state. By contrast, ICESCR entails the state.

Only secondarily, as a result of pressure from the socialist democratic South and the communist East, has the focus on economic, social, and cultural rights become a priority in the West. On December 19, 1966, ICESCR was offered for signature. It entered into force on January 3, 1976, and gave legitimate authority to Articles 22 through 27 of UDHR. These "second generation" rights are essentially responses to the abuses and misuses of capitalist development. In his *The Real World of Democracy*, C. B. MacPherson talks about those abuses and misuses:

> [A] capitalist market society necessarily involves a net transfer of part of the powers of some men to others. The politics of choice and the society of competition do contain, and generally conceal, a compulsive transfer of powers which is a diminution of the human essence.[46]

His recommendation:

> [T]ell your politicians that the free way of life depends, to an extent they have not yet dreamed of, on the Western nations remedying the inequality of human rights as between ourselves and the poor nations. Nothing less than massive aid, which will enable the poor nations to lift themselves to recognizable human equality, will now conserve the moral stature and the power of the liberal-democracies.[47]

The operation of the capitalist system in a country that has, through the logic of its development, chosen this economic alternative is one issue. The imposition of the capitalist system on wholly unwilling states is another matter entirely. The struggle of those countries emerging from colonialism and the imperialism of the West to throw off the shroud of the system that was a tool of their oppression gives them a very different perspective on what is necessary to a satisfactory life. ICESCR fulfills those requirements. ICESCR constitutes a counterpoint to ICCPR's "first generation" rights. The tension between proponents of a primary emphasis on liberty and those who advocate an ongoing struggle for equity has been a major source of contention among the nations of the world, with the West opting for liberty as a primary value and less affluent nations (understandably) choosing to focus on equity and the collective good. For this reason, as late as February 23, 1993, at a meeting in Washington, D.C., the NGO Coalition recommendations to the representatives to the World Conference on Human Rights[48] included the injunction to the powerful nations of the West to "[r]ecognize the indivisibility and equality of all human rights; economic, social, cultural, political and civil." Somewhere within this fundamental tension between the "first" and "third" world and first and second generations of human rights, one would expect to find protection for women. Yet, as indicated previously, such is not the case.

Among the primary concerns of the United Nations was support for countries that had achieved their freedom from colonization but had yet to acquire the resources and the autonomy to be actually "self-determining." This "third generation" of rights is foreshadowed by Article 28 of UDHR: "everyone is entitled to a social and international order in which the rights set forth in this Declaration can be fully realized." The distinction between second and third generation rights is that second generation rights provide government assurance of basic human requirements and third generation rights promote broader more encompassing rights such as rights to peace and development. Both generations challenge the West to move beyond first generation rights. According to southern and eastern states, first generation rights fail to recognize the importance of the state as a facilitator in the provision of material human needs. Liberty, according to proponents of second and third generation rights, is not of value if one's basic needs are not met. Liberty is, therefore, not necessarily viewed as outside the definition of human rights but is assigned lower status; it is a long-term goal. MacPherson would agree:

> The implacable force in the drama of liberal society was scarcity in relation to limited desire. It was scarcity and unlimited desire that made the drama, and while it lasted it was tragedy. But now we can see it for what it has become, melodrama. Scarcity in relation to unlimited desire can now be seen for what it is, merely the villain in a melodrama, who can be disposed of before the play is finished. We can begin to recognize now that the vision of scarcity in relation to unlimited desire was a creation of capitalist market society. Certainly before the advent of that society, nobody assumed that unlimited desire was a natural and proper attribute of the human being. You do not find it in Aristotle or St. Thomas Aquinas.[49]

MacPherson goes on to say that the concepts "scarcity" and "unlimited desire" were used in concert to justify unlimited acquisition, and that man is not, in fact, an "infinitely desirous creature." In most advanced societies, we already create more commodities and new capital than we can use. Ultimately, it is not the creation of commodities and capital that is necessary, but their equitable distribution.

The "Will" to Human Rights
in the United States System

Until recently, U.S. failure to offer systemic support for international protection of human rights was greatly influenced by bipolar tension with the Soviet Union. The political "combatants" were each determined to preserve their own allies regardless of those allies' human rights records. The primary goal of each—the exportation of its own particular ideology—was paramount. These tensions also served to obscure the characteristics and dynamics of the U.S. culture, which are only becoming evident in the aftermath of the Cold War. Therefore, the balance of this chapter examines the specific actions and reactions of each of the branches of the American government.

Just prior to the end of the Cold War, the Carter administration attempted, but failed, to assert a strong policy on human rights. He was the first American president to advocate human rights as of primary importance in setting and carrying out foreign policy. Because there were no (or few) precedents for this kind of behavior by an American president, his human rights policies were highly publicized and much was made of each situation in which they seemingly failed.[50] That Jimmy Carter was unsuccessful in his attempt to promote human rights was neither the acid test for the efficacy of human rights as a fundamental component of foreign policy, nor was it simply an indication of his ineffectiveness in carrying out his own policy. In a very real way, the Carter administration's failure is an indictment of the foreign policy-making system that continues to emphasize a will to power rather than a will to human equity.[51] Carter was in the unenviable position of attempting to advance a coherent policy on human rights in the waning though still turbulent years of the Cold War. When confronted with the option of greater U.S. involvement in treaty ratification or simply allowing the matter to drop, the default (or knee-jerk) political response of the nation was to protect U.S. autonomy.

A question, thus, presented itself in the aftermath of the Cold War: Why, in the absence of the paranoia that pervaded the Cold War era, does the United States still not advance a clear policy of promotion and support for those states that honor the human rights of their citizens? Earlier in this chapter, the question of increasing internationalization of corporate interests was proposed. Another possible response is that the political climate remains one of suspicion and guardedness. With no popular push to alter policy, subsequent administrations have focused almost exclusively on military intervention in state-to-state disputes and military aid, usually to the democratizing faction, in state domestic conflicts. Thus, despite U.S. rhetoric around the emphasis on globalization of liberty and equality and on humanitarian intervention abroad, the United States has yet to form a coherent and consistent foreign policy on human rights. The question remains, however, why this phenomenon, which has been evident in U.S. behavior on the subject of human rights treaty ratification since the 1950s, endures.[52] There are several additional reasons, some more evident than others, why this is the case.

Initial U.S. involvement in establishing definitions of human rights abuse and its own participation in the development of international human rights instruments did not, as one might reasonably have expected, result in wholehearted incorporation of human rights instruments within its own social and legal systems. In the 1940s, the United States considered itself the sanctuary for all who sought freedom and prosperity. As long as Cold War paranoia pervaded the United States, its use of military or economic power to maintain its preeminence in the world was justified based on fear of the "spread of communist oppression." That fear is no longer a compelling one. The opportunity to focus more specifically on human rights abuses has offered itself in increasingly less complicated ways, especially since the end of the Cold War.

The end to bipolar tension, in and of itself, clarifies and rearranges the priorities in many state interactions. U.S. standing in these altered world relationships requires—under relatively peaceful conditions—a certain willingness on the part of the United States to involve itself in the full support and development of United Nations influence. The arbitrary use of power— either military or economic—(if it was ever justified) is no longer an isolated option. Traditionally, U.S. aid and military support has been afforded to states that (1) are of economic interest to the United States, (2) have chosen to ally themselves against the spread of Communism, and (3) are supported by multinational corporations and banking interests. The attitudes of the current chair of the Senate Foreign Relations Committee are consistent with these priorities. Though the attitudes of Jesse Helms do not necessarily represent the sentiment of the entire Congress, the recent tenor at the national level does not bode well for the promotion of human rights. On the contrary, greater influence of conservatism in Congress in the 1990s has tended toward even greater isolationism. In fact, many Republican representatives do not have passports and wear this fact as a badge of honor. Yet, the future of human rights protections may well lie with this conservative body. David Forsythe strongly implies that it does. He claims that, to date, the future of U.S. commitment to international human rights standards has hinged on the intermittent attention of Congress and its ability to "ride out the storms" of the inherent vagaries of successive administrations.[53]

Past administrations have not accepted the role of change-agent in international human rights policy. Even those who recognized the need faltered before the weight of economic interests and the skepticism inherent in international relations, both theoretically and practically. For example, Carter was condemned for his insistence on making human rights a priority in a world that was still polarized by the Cold War. His seemingly erratic, because unsupported, emphasis on human rights appeared to the American public (no less to foreign leaders) to be a sign of indecisiveness and weak resolve. Neither could the American public rely on him to act, as had many of his predecessors (and have his successors), with cold calculation, through military force. His administration was torn, as no other had ever been, by his attempts to alter what had become a national truth. His effectiveness as a leader was seriously undermined by his inability to present a compelling argument for the advancement of human rights in the face of this country's continued acceptance, if not valorization, of military action as a resolution to foreign policy problems. The continued reliance of the United States on military force was clearly evident in the waning years of the Cold War—the attack on Grenada, the bombing and strafing of Libya, and the removal of the President of Nicaragua through covert military action—and seems to have remained operative subsequent to that era in light of (among other instances) the wars in the Persian Gulf and in Kosovo.

Congress and NGOs: A Political Shell Game?

It seems ironic that, despite its greater conservatism, Congress is the body on which Americans—and perhaps many others—must rely for progressive changes in U.S. foreign policy on human rights. In contrast to the less than encouraging response of successive administrations, the work of NGOs has been supported more consistently by Congress. Congress has been forced, by the lack of explicit leadership of past presidents and the continued reticence of the courts to base decisions on international treaty, to assume a leadership role in shaping U.S. policy on international human rights. David Forsythe reported in 1987 that "Congress, not the Executive, initiated the idea of a positive use of economic aid linked to human rights." But Forsythe is also clear that Congress lacks "the attention span, the will power and the consensus for effective oversight that would implement the original Congressional intent."[54] Yet, because there are NGOs willing to implement the programs, Congress is not required to have a long memory. Congress need neither concern itself with seeking out data on human rights violations nor with interpreting that data. That activity is the purview of NGOs. The cooperative efforts of Congress and NGOs will be necessary to carry out policies that initiate and promote international human rights protections. One significant drawback is that Congress, while it is willing to promote human rights and adherence to agreements elsewhere, is not willing to put real emphasis on ratification of the same treaties by the United States.

Nonetheless, Congress can act as a more effective change-agent internationally, because there is less critical emphasis placed on decisions by Congress (which is not perceived as a potentially coherent, strategy-setting body within the area of foreign relations) than on the executive. Intervention by Congress could be described as a type of "Track II Diplomacy."[55] Vamik Volkan uses this concept in advocating less high-profile, high-intensity negotiation of critical, yet extremely sensitive, issues. His contention is that little may be achieved between high-profile actors in the intense spotlight of international speculation—that the real work of diplomacy is accomplished by those who are less apt to act in an effort to "save face." Additionally, implementation of congressional decisions by NGOs has the effect of removing the activity yet another step from the executive and, again, the resulting distance reduces the implied threat to the targeted country's regime. But this argument centers on the need to encourage behavior in other states and again sidesteps the need for ratification in the United States.

In terms of the incorporation of international treaties within the U.S. system, Congress has accomplished little more than have successive administrations. The only positive result is that the lack of effectiveness at the highest levels has strengthened the network of NGOs, just as lack of direction by the executive forced NGOs' relationship with Congress. But, no treaty is ratified without extensive lobby, education, and justification by the executive branch. Without executive support treaties generally languish.

Judicial Involvement and Interpretation

The courts' reliance on human rights law has been limited also. It seems that handing down rulings based on international treaty law would "open a can of worms," as it were. Despite this reluctance, one case in particular has "helped to set U.S. judicial policy on a course of reform."[56] In 1979, the case of the torture and murder of Joelita Filartiga in Paraguay was tried in a United States court. That the case was heard at all in a U.S. court established the precedent (in the United States) that each nation may award standing to individual claims of "crimes against humanity." Just as the tribunal at Nuremberg had established the responsibility of the international community to protect the human rights of citizens, this case made the assertion on behalf of an individual and necessitated an individual state response to a claim by a non-national. Because the perpetrator had already been tried in

Paraguay, Dr. Filartiga, Joelita's father, could only file civil charges in U.S. court. The case, *Filartiga* v. *Pena-Irala* (1979), "made clear that abusers of internationally defined human rights from other countries who find themselves in the United States can be held liable for damages."

Richard Claude asserts:

> Finally, *Filartiga* v. *Pena* should have an important impact on the prospects for international human rights enforcement. International law and its implementation [are] based on a horizontal power structure with no central enforcing authority . . . [thus] the issue was crystallized as one of the progressive applications of international law in general and of the application of international law by national courts in particular.[57]

The Filartiga case may well have set a precedent in the U.S. judicial system, but U.S. legislation on broader issues is necessary to bring other, equally critical, issues before the court. In the Filartiga case the U.S. court was responding to a suit brought by a foreign national. The court was not responding to clearly defined, existing U.S. legislation, but to a general outcry in the form of amicus curiae briefs supporting the Filartigas claim under the U.S. Constitution given U.S. commitment to international human rights. The amicus curiae briefs served to "challenge as anachronistic the perception that problems arising under the international law of human rights may not be dealt with by domestic courts."[58] The claimants in the Filartiga case were successful, but the hue and cry that accompanied this case is relatively unprecedented and cannot be relied upon to find justice in all, or even similar, cases. The U.S. domestic court ruling on this case notwithstanding, the issues brought before the courts are a far cry from protection of women's human rights, though some cases may provide a basis for similar claims.

International Cooperation:
U.S. Reconstitution of Rhetoric and Reality

The United States is the only remaining superpower. The Cold War is over and we are facing an exhilarating future. It is now time for the United States to reconnect with its fundamental conceptions of human being; those conceptions that might have flourished in the absence of elevation of capitalism to the level of ideology. If we rely, as Soros claims, too heavily on the global market as the connector between and among nations of the world, we forego the opportunity to establish a global open society. As an economic system, capitalism may be exemplary. As a system of social organization for the future, it is as totalizing and oppressive as the worst dictatorship. Therefore, we must continue to examine the tension between liberty and equality, not as a choice between possessive individualism and tedious, procedural democratic decision-making that stifles creativity, but as an integrated whole. According to Soros, if we fail to make the transition to a global open society and continue to rely upon a global market as the fundamental connector,

> we are left with the impression that people are guided by their self-interest as isolated individuals. In reality, people are social animals: the survival of the fittest must involve cooperation as well as competition. There is a common flaw in market fundamentalism, geopolitical realism, and vulgar social Darwinism: the disregard of altruism and cooperation.

One way for the United States to begin the process of transition is to reinforce the faltering influence of the United Nations; first, by paying its dues and, then, by taking an active role in advancing human rights agendas. Another is to offer unambivalent support to those countries that adhere to the letter and the intent of the human rights treaties to which they are party and to honor the collectively determined sanctions imposed on those who do not. Finally, the United States must lead the world in encouraging and supporting state initiated development projects. It must also involve itself in modifying the benefits realized by multinational corporations who exploit their relative access to cheap labor and raw materials. One way of accomplishing this is by cooperating in the imposition of restrictions that ultimately reward equalization of the global economy.

A propitious beginning to U.S. acceptance of its altered relationships with other, particularly non-Western nations, would be ratification of ICESCR and CEDAW, which could initiate national debate on the critical issues that face us in the coming century. It is not the end of history, as Francis Fukuyama would have it, but the beginning of a new era, because, as Donnelly says quite succinctly: "The moral universality of human rights, which has been codified in a strong set of authoritative international norms, must be realized through the particularities of national action.[59]

Chapter 5 🐛

The Injustice of Equality

Women, International Human Rights, and Liberal Democracy in America

> Domination arises out of an inability to recognize, appreciate and nurture differences, not out of a failure to see everyone as the same. Indeed, the need to see everyone the same in order to accord them dignity and respect is an expression of the problem, not a cure for it.[1]
>
> —Jane Flax, 1992

Women face limitations within U.S. social, economic, and legal systems that have precluded their full involvement in the construction of instruments and institutions that directly affect their lives. The limitations that women experience are not a result of invidious manipulation of the institutions of the state system, but are a fundamental failure of the liberal democratic system in the United States to address the needs of those who are necessarily marginalized by the traditionally white male-privileging structure. As a direct result of this normative construction of civil society, opportunities to effect salutary change in these systems continue to be unavailable to women, as women.[2]

This chapter moves beyond the specific failures of liberal democracy in the United States and suggests alternatives to the American model in globalizing concern for women's human rights. The fundamental argument is that the United States has inherent systemic flaws in terms of its provisions for women. The argument in this chapter is based on three assumptions. As it was conceived and has developed in the United States, liberal democracy: (1) has precluded women's full involvement in the political processes that directly affect the quality of their lives; (2) does not represent a case of invidious manipulation of the system, but faithfully outlines the fundamental assumptions and dynamics inherent to the development of this particular system; and (3) can be identified as peculiar to the United States.

Various (particularly) Western democracies have developed under what appear to be quite similar conditions, yet, the United States is unique in its self-conscious view of its own history and relative global power:

> As first a reluctant great power and then a more willing super power, the United States has faced the traditional conflict between commitment to human values and exercise of power for other interests. Equally important in an interdependent and nonhegemonic world, the United States has painfully discovered that its version of human rights is not the same as that of the rest of the world.[3]

As Forsythe suggests, the U.S. system, because of its resistance to the expansion of human rights definitions, remains a relative outsider in the ongoing development of human rights instruments.[4] Such isolationism inhibits U.S. collaboration on the subject of universally agreed upon human values. At the same time, U.S. unwillingness to be informed by international agreements projects the image of a discrete, elitist entity that views ratification of international human rights treaties as unnecessary to its own progress; as necessary only for other, "lesser" regimes.

Though I argue in chapter 3 that ratification of the International Bill of Human Rights (IBHR) is essential to the development of the world community, this does not mean that solutions to the problem of women's exclusion may be found through unreflexive recourse to international norms and standards in the form of IBHR. Neither do I suggest, for that matter, that true equity for women would be achieved through simple ratification of CEDAW. Although nonratification of CEDAW constitutes a critical failure of the United States in its duty to its citizens, ratification would not radically change the nature of U.S. public policy. Ratification would constitute a symbolic reaffirmation by the United States that citizens (1) have rights that are beyond the authority of the state to confer or rescind and (2) that those rights are universal. Ratification of CEDAW would provide a framework for state recognition and protection of those rights, and would clarify parameters. Second, but not less important, ratification promotes global cooperation and facilitates global scrutiny.

If we, as a world community, are to prepare the way for a peaceful and productive global future, then each state must begin by requiring the optimum in justice and fairness of itself under a system of common and reciprocal scrutiny. Preparing for the future means, precisely, recognizing and being willing to correct the inequities and shortcomings of the present. However, the purpose of correction is not served simply through ratification of the major human rights treaties. The covenants that were specifically designed to address fundamental human rights issues—the International Covenant on Civil and Political Rights (ICCPR) and the International Covenant on Economic, Social, and Cultural Rights (ICESCR)—are, themselves, flawed in terms of their capacity to alleviate harms to women. Their failure to alleviate those harms is not, however, a result of their departure from the tenets of Western liberalism. Though necessary as a framework for global communication and cooperation, these treaties function as a reinscription—at the international level—of the very conditions within the United States that have served to exclude women for centuries.

ICESCR moves closer to the protection of women's human rights in that ratification and meaningful incorporation of ICESCR would require stronger commitments to programs of redistribution and economic assurance. But these commitments are no more than what would be available in a strong welfare state. Further, ratification and meaningful incorporation of CEDAW represent a commitment by a progressive state, which, upon recognition that its systems and institutions inordinately and unjustifiably privilege one segment of society over others, attempts to alter conditions of discrimination and marginalization. In, chapter 1, I argue that CEDAW is an instrument of *human* rights protection and as such questions foundational issues that have long plagued the United States in terms of its attitudes toward state-conferred civil rights. Whether justified or not, the attitude toward extension of civil rights to blacks and women in this country has been viewed as offering special protection; unwarranted preference.[5] Given the conservative mood of the country in 1999,[6] critics of affirmative action might well ask "if human rights are the issue, why is it necessary to ratify a treaty concerned specifically with women's rights?"

As argued at length in chapter 3, neither ICCPR nor ICESCR extends protections in such a way as to penetrate substantially the public/private boundary that serves to invisibilize women. Despite the difficulties that may arise in U.S. ratification and incorporation of ICESCR—particularly in view of U.S. commitment to "free market" enterprise as the very foundation of the liberal tradition—neither ICESCR nor ICCPR address private relationships of the individual or group that are reinforced, even perpetuated, by the state. Consequently, the tensions that do exist between the United States and the international covenants do not include significant tension with regard to women's human rights. In fact, incorporation of mainstream human rights treaties alone provides virtually no protection for women, as women.

Marguerite Bouvard makes the point that is central to international concern for women:

> While most abuses of women fall within the purview of the Universal Declaration of Human Rights, adopted in 1948, such violations have tended to be ignored by governments. This is because human rights abuses, such as domestic violence, occur within what typically has been defined as "the private sphere" and are therefore not recognized as legal offenses. . . . Domestic violence, rape, the trafficking in women, genital mutilation, female infanticide, sexual harassment, pornography, and reproductive rights have not been included within the agenda of the more established human rights organizations because the crimes are not perpetrated by public authorities.[7]

Bouvard's argument is that the interpretation and development of human rights law, as set forth in ICCPR and ICESCR, reinscribe systemic (state) indifference to the harms that are peculiar to women, as women. Yet, these instruments do extend beyond the negative rights protections provided in the liberal tradition. It is ICESCR's extension beyond negative rights protections that brings it into conflict with U.S. liberal legal tradition.

Granted, the basis for international human rights claims is found in the Western, liberal ideology of freedom, equality, and the moral priority of the individual. In fact, women enjoy political and economic access in Western cultures that is denied them in various other countries. Further, the access that women have achieved is a tribute to the corrigibility of liberalism as well as to decades of struggle by women to attain some measure of equity. Yet, this very same liberalism—as it has been defined and practiced in the West—continues to fail, in a fundamental way, to address the harms suffered by women and others who do not fit the traditional description of "full citizen."[8] But what manner of modification might be possible?

Clearly, one cannot argue that U.S. ratification of CEDAW would magically eliminate the oppression and exclusion of women worldwide. However, as newly democratizing states are attempting to fashion their specific regimes around various forms of democracy, concern should center around the relative corrigibility of the liberal democratic system. Ultimately, one of the most important challenges facing the world today is modification of the forms that liberal democracy takes.

There are three distinct, yet related, truths that reflect the immediacy and criticality of this challenge for women: (1) women remain primarily responsible for the birth, health, education, and development of the children of each nation; (2) women do not experience the freedom to engage fully in political, institutional, and educational processes that have the potential to create optimum conditions for their own and their children's development;

and (3) there is a fleeting window of opportunity—afforded by the present conditions of restructuring—that offers the political space to effect change. The following sections are an effort to identify possible obstructions to meeting that challenge within the U.S. system.

Systemic Realities

The assumption that pervades the American consciousness is that liberal democracy operating within a market economy is *the* superior system of state governance and social equity. Moreover, Americans assume that the coincidence of a market economy and a liberal democratic system also constitutes "the best" sociopolitical and economic structure. The argument in chapter 4 is that these assumptions have been somewhat reinforced (though not as thoroughly as some might imagine) by the fact that, following the dissolution of the Soviet Union and the collapse of communist (and other) regimes in much of Eastern Europe and Africa, many states have turned to either liberal or social democratic systems. Yet, almost without exception, the women of these states have reported not an increased recognition of their contributions as citizens but rather a significant loss of freedom and autonomy as a result of the economic and public/political processes of reconstruction within their countries.[9] The reports clearly indicate problems with both liberal democratic and social democratic systems. This chapter focuses exclusively on problems peculiar to the liberal democratic system in the United States.

Women's experiences are almost as varied within the United States as they are globally. Therefore, given the potential influence of the United States as a model for democracies in their formative stages, it becomes necessary to explore the effects of the U.S. liberal democratic system on women. Conversely, and just as critically, the experience of women in newly democratized states may point to fundamental issues to be addressed by women in the United States:

> A further breach in the dichotomy between public and private on the international level (i.e., between international and domestic law) has been raised by legal theorists in the Third World who question any metaphysical disengagement of the state from historical, economic, and political realities.[10]

According to Zillah Eisenstein:

> If really new ground is to be broken, the insights of Western feminist theorists must refocus the discussion of democracy to include the racialized relations of sex and gender and familial structures and how those relations affect the individual and the economy.[11]

This complementary activity entails not simply analysis and remediation within each state, but a universal recognition of the national and international complexity of common issues.[12] Eisenstein's insights offer a view of domestic realities that are closely related to international realities. Her refocused conception of liberal democracy forces one to consider not just the economic and legal relationship of the individual to the state, but also the changing relationships of individuals in the community to one another and to the state.

> So where are we? Someplace between liberal and socialist visions of patriarchal society, where the tension between individual freedom and gender equality is not resolved. This place—in-between—is traversed by democratic theory. This place is where we must finally recognize the heterogeneity of power and dislocate the economy as the core of democracy.[13]

Although it alleviates some of the human rights abuses experienced by those who are oppressed under less egalitarian regimes, liberal democracy in conjunction with a market economy fails to address the situation of those within the state who have been, historically and globally, denied full access to the institutions and instruments that regulate their lives. Therefore, far from having reached "the end of history,"[14] it behooves us to regain some sense of history in order to refresh our collective memories about the primary purpose of community and to review our own development over time.

In his *The Life and Times of Liberal Democracy*, C. B. MacPherson poses the question, "Why look at successive models [of liberal democracy]?" His response is:

> The simplest reason is that using successive models reduces the risk of myopia in looking ahead. It is all too easy, in using a single model, to block off future paths; all too easy to fall into thinking that liberal democracy, now that we have attained it, by whatever stages, is fixed in its present mould.[15]

Many in the United States have fallen victim to this myopic view. It has led to the assumption that liberal democracy, as it exists in the United States, is sufficiently perfected; that the search is over. On the contrary, Eisenstein suggests that considerable modification is necessary to eradicate the marginalizing effects that are inherent to the system as it exists. She envisions a "radicalization" of liberal democracy. Her perspective is particularly helpful in outlining possible alterations:

> For me democracy means individual freedom, which requires privacy of and for bodies, as well as social, economic, political, sexual, racial and gender

equality. It does not mean rugged individualism as envisioned by Hobbes or Locke, or by John Stuart Mill, for that matter. It is a commitment to the individual, nevertheless—to an individual who has social connections and commitments but also autonomy.[16]

Some have made the argument that liberalism in its pure form is not limiting, and that, conceptually, it would not have affected women as it subsequently has.[17] This argument has little relevance in the investigation of a particular system. The application of any abstract concept is necessarily limited by the perspectives of the architects of each specific model. In the United States, that application is defined by a particular form of liberalism improvised and enforced by "the few" in the absence of significant regard for dissimilarly constructed or positioned "other(s)."

Yet, this form of exclusion is not unusual, nor is it unique to the United States. In fact, according to David Campbell, this dimension of being is inescapable:

> no "body" could be without it. Whether we are speaking of personal or collective identity, "it" is not fixed by nature, given by God, or planned by intentional behavior. Rather identity is constituted in relation to difference. Equally, difference is constituted in relation to identity, such that the problematic of identity/difference contains no foundations that are prior to, or outside of, its operation.... Moreover, this constitution of identity is achieved through the inscription of boundaries that serve to demarcate an inside from an outside, a self from an other, a domestic from a foreign.[18]

Because, the operation of this self/other dynamic is present in Campbell's account, at all levels of interaction, it constitutes a particularly ubiquitous phenomenon in our lives. But, more importantly, he argues that the phenomenon in itself is not harmful if difference does not equal domination. His assertion accords well with Robin West's view:

> Hierarchical relationships can strengthen our autonomy and leave us better off if they help us grow, develop talents, or improve our mental health, physical health, store of knowledge or wisdom. They weaken us and leave us worse off if they render us dependent on an unreliable or untrustworthy source of information, if they divest us of the power to engage in essential human activities, or if they deprive us of self-respect or the ability to make independent moral judgments.[19]

West's argument is a consequentialist one. She reminds us that it is not the theoretical definitions of our institutions that we experience, it is the practical operation and effects of those institutions that augment or detract from our well-being and autonomy. Therefore, that liberalism in some "pure" form would not have affected women as it subsequently has is not pertinent here. What is pertinent is that justice is not possible if difference is coexistent with domination in legal, political, economic, and social realms. In support of this argument, Jane Flax notes women's experience within Western culture: "Within western culture differences appear to generate and are certainly used to justify hierarchies and relations of domination including gender-based (or gender-ascribed) ones."[20] Yet, both West and Flax take the argument a bit farther. In their corresponding judgment, the demands of feminist liberal legal theory for recognition of women's equality under the existing system deny *actual* differences in women's and men's experience of harm. Demands that women be considered "equal" to men, by their accounts, miss the point.[21] Further, as non-Western feminists have argued for the last two decades, the differences in the lived experiences of women themselves must be a primary consideration in the development of any global effort on behalf of women.

In the preceding chapters, I have argued that the U.S. system fails to provide a model for the globalization of concern for women's human rights, and that interpretations of the International Bill of Human Rights are inadequate in their provisions for women and that women themselves have had to struggle to overcome the differences that have divided them. This final chapter examines the specific problems and endeavors to point out ways of addressing those problems.

Thus, this is not an examination of liberalism in its "pure" form. The argument is that, comparatively, liberal democracy in the United States does trump other existing systems in terms of its provisions for citizens' freedom, equality of opportunity, and well-being. But, despite this (some would say, exemplary) performance, we have not reached the "end of history"—as Fukuyama would have it. We are simply, because of significant global restructuring of systems, enjoying the "political space" to investigate the limitations of one peculiar form of liberalism.

Liberalism

Liberalism does not, in all places and at all times, constitute the identical concept. Despite similarities, there are differing "strains" of liberalism among Western states. The various forms that liberalism takes embody distinct characteristics that are peculiar, for example, to France, Germany, Britain and the United States.[22] The unique historical development of each state (for example, the influences of certain philosophies over others and the constraints of specific geopolitical environments) serves to create very clear distinctions between and among these so-called liberal states. Yet, John

Gray's definition of liberalism is helpful in setting forth the general claims that liberalism makes:

> It is *individualist*, in that it asserts the moral primacy of the person against the claims of any social collectivity; *egalitarian*, inasmuch as it confers on all men the same moral status and denies the relevance to legal or political order of differences in moral worth among human beings; *universalist*, affirming the moral unity of the human species and according a secondary importance to specific historic associations and cultural forms; and *meliorist*, in its affirmation of the corrigibility and improvability of all social institutions and political arrangements.[23]

Admittedly, the distinctions between and among liberal democracies are subtle and the claim here is not that other liberal democratic systems do not exclude or oppress women. The argument that women are oppressed elsewhere, under various other liberal democratic systems, is extraneous to the issues addressed here. In fact, other models based on the liberal tradition and its provisions may also struggle under various claims of systemic failure. However, the responsibility that the United States faces is to analyze limitations that are peculiar to its own system.

For decades, women in the United States have struggled for equality, but equality has been measured by the traditional, male standard. Consequently, women's entrance into the public space has meant adopting characteristics and qualities defined by the system as legitimate, and "leaving behind" in the private space those incommensurate parts of the self. In other words, legitimacy in the public space has required women to operate as if they embodied the characteristics traditionally privileged in the public space. However, women have come to realize that to gain access as women, it is incumbent upon them to gain that access without denying their differences from men, but also without denying their differences from one another. Consequently, in recent years, women have come to realize the importance of embodying and expressing the gendered-raced-ethnic[24] self in the "public space."

The ever-increasing realization that characteristics and qualities of "otherness" must necessarily be part of our contribution to the public areas of life has meant asking some very difficult questions about the standards and values of the public space:

> Feminist theorists search for explanations of gender and women's experience, reasons to and methods of struggle against domination, ways to understand our own complicity in them and evidence that struggle against domination by ourselves and others is worthwhile.[25]

Much contemporary feminist debate has centered around resolving this critical dilemma. The inclusion of women, as women, in the public space and addressing their "difference" has meant investigating the boundaries between the public and private areas of life. Further, as recognition of various differences becomes the norm rather than the exception in the United States, it has been necessary to pose questions with regard to the meaning of culture, if the "culture" does not reflect the actual composition of the state.[26] Continued systemic exclusion of "others" from the public space coupled with inherent asymmetries in power arrangements remains a prevalent issue.[27] As a result, despite U.S. claims to exemplify human rights practices, the United States fails to serve as a propitious model for globalizing concern for women's human rights.

Those who are critical of an increased focus on women's human rights in the United States claim that full unreserved ratification of CEDAW would entail the destruction of (1) fundamental forms of organization and (2) the ostensibly unrestricted operation of democratic processes.[28] Such resistance serves only to sustain definitions that are no longer representative (if they ever were) of the cultural composition of the United States. However, dissolution of the ideologically sustained rigid boundaries between public and private areas of life does render problematic traditional liberal democratic structures and traditional (also traditional feminist) liberal legal thought. The central question that arises is the efficacy of a rights discourse in attempting to "reveal" women's oppression.

Public/Private Dichotomy:
Does a Rights Discourse Suffice?

The idea of a private sphere unregulated—virtually untouched—by government is a direct result of a Lockean understanding of individualism. Locke's treatise on government represents the fundamental basis for rights to privacy in the United States. His argument is that in the absence of a very clearly delineated sphere of privacy, the state would have the capacity to grant (and, thus, the capacity to rescind) rights that individuals already embodied prior to the creation of the state. According to Locke's account, human reason and a direct connection with "his" God, afford "him" the capacity to direct "his" own life. To that end, Locke's construction of the civil society creates a very clear boundary between what is public and what is private. Yet, the "he" of Locke's understanding is not the (ostensibly) neutral "he," but a distinctly gendered "he," which by some magic is later transformed into the neutral, standardized "he." The myth of the ostensibly gender-neutral "he" is played out in American history in various ways and is at the very heart of the argument for women's human rights. As a matter of fact, in the early years of the struggle for women's rights in the United States, the myth of the neutral "he" profoundly affected and severely delimited women's consciousness of oppressive conditions.[29] The current question that arises for women is, "Can a rights discourse serve as a vehicle for expression of women's claims?" There is—even among women—no singular response to this question.[30]

The struggle to define a "woman's perspective" on a given policy issue is complicated by the various attitudes of women themselves with regard to what they term "rights." That women's definitions frequently come into conflict on the subject of rights, is primarily a function of differing emphases on traditional interpretations and expectations. These definitions are also profoundly affected by disparities in class, race, ethnicity, and sexual orientation. Traditional (we can now say "traditional") feminist theory—particularly feminist liberal legal theory in the United States—has come to be viewed as reductive and exclusionary. The clearly articulated "voice" of the feminist movement in the early 1960s was middle class, white, and heterosexual. For various reasons, the movement was very narrowly defined. The primary reason was that the larger system could (with the least disruption) accomodate women who had the available time, education, and psychological makeup required for organized activism. Yet, due in no small measure to the globalization of concern for women's rights in the 1970s,[31] women have become much more aware of their own diversity. Nevertheless, problems persist. A woman may endeavor to express her own unique "standpoint," but must constitute her argument in such a way as to be heard within the "dominant" discourse—whether mainstream or feminist.[32]

Within feminist thought in the United States prior to the 1970s, the prevailing ideal had been the experience of individuality: to be situated "as men" in relation to the state. Women's reality until that point had been sharply circumscribed: Only through her very particularly proscribed attachments (1) did she exist in the public sphere and (2) were her "natural" or ascribed roles fulfilled. Her attachment to her father/husband was fundamental to her protection by the state. Her biological, as well as socially ascribed, attachment to her children was ostensibly a private matter not to be interfered with by the state, but her "privacy" has only recently been extended to control over her own body, which had been seen previously as an instrument for fulfilling the fundamental goals of the state.[33] Therefore, as a presence primarily in her relation to the individual male and recognized functionally as an instrument of the state, she was not afforded the position of moral primacy enjoyed by franchised males. As fundamentally attached, she did not experience the protection of the (individualist) state in the same way as men. This was especially true since her "attachments" were circumscribed by state-mandated institutions and any "deviation" from state-proscribed connections was not recognized as "legitimate" by the state.[34]

Thus, women's attempts to relate to the state "as men" forced them to deny essential pieces of themselves in order to fit the preexisting model of "full" citizen. What are women to do if emulation of the male model serves only to bind them still further? Can women (who are not individual) be served by a "rights discourse"?

The position of women in the rights debate is neither singular nor is it unambiguous. A critical area of the debate centers around the question of negative and positive rights. For example, a woman's decisions concerning her own body (though now legally hers) are circumscribed in various ways. This is especially true in the experience of young, poor, unwed mothers, of nonwhite groups, and/or those in nonheterosexual relationships, whose reality is quite different from that described by the dominant discourses.[35]

According to the precepts of liberal democracy, citizens have free choice in private matters (without regard, at this point, for the multitude of ways the state circumscribes private choice). This right to (private) choice constitutes a (negative) protection against state interference. Thus, women's negative right to choice concerning abortion is legally mandated. Yet, for poor women access to certain services may be mitigated by the necessary positive intervention (either in the form of insurance or social welfare programs) by the state to fund the required medical procedure. Many states have denied access to public funds in procedures to end pregnancy. Denying access to public funds for a legal procedure amounts to an unwarranted distinction between those who can afford to make autonomous decisions and those who must allow the state to determine their futures. In effect, if not in fact, the state owns the body of a poor woman when her right to choose is entirely circumscribed by her ability to pay.

The very idea of a woman's right to her own body raises the question of individuality: Is a pregnant woman "individual"? What issues are raised in asking the question? Does viewing pregnant women as individual (1) support a state interest in circumscribing her right to choose and (2) legitimize the effort to discontinue state support for abortion procedures? How does this conflict with the idea that poor women who have babies while on welfare are criticized for "manipulating" the system to enrich themselves and therefore should be penalized?

As citizens within a system that is thus constructed, we are extremely schizophrenic about the "welfare state." The insistence on maintaining the facade of personal responsibility is so seamlessly ingrained in this country's psychological development that even proponents of a stronger welfare state are influenced—sometimes quelled—by its power. This situation creates what amounts to a double-bind for a poor, single woman with children on welfare. In an individualist, predominantly patriarchal society, the presumption remains that a "family" requires a male (individual) head-of-household. Women who for whatever reason are not legally attached to a man, experience negative freedoms (that is, the right to be left alone) in a situation that requires both the negative right of an individual to make choices about her own body *and* positive action by the state to ensure access to the procedures that make her choice a reality. She, therefore, is treated as an individual (within the civil construction of "individual") without the benefit of preexisting institutions that promote and support the development of the requisite autonomy, legal status, or cultural impetus to acquire and develop said autonomy. According to Virginia Sapiro:

> Social policy has assumed that women are not autonomous individuals and moral agents, but that they live contingent lives. With specific regard to their economic lives, their ability to provide for themselves and others is supposed to be contingent upon whether others around them need their caring services. Choice as a moral agent is missing.[36]

Nature of Men and Women

The boundary between the public and private spheres of life continues to be an essential characteristic of liberal society. In order to be recognized as a "full citizen" one requires agency within both spheres. In contemporary society, can this agency be denied to women? Because involvement in the public space would detract from her legitimate role as caregiver, it is a fundamental tenet of liberal democracy, as it has been conceived and subsequently developed, that women not be recognized as full citizens. In none of the early theoretical constructions of civil society were women identified as agents, neither agents of their estates nor of their own bodies. Locke and Rousseau saw women as adjunct to their male relatives and as fulfilling a state function. Hobbes did not mention them at all. John Stuart Mill argued that women must be allowed, if they wished (and Mill was very clear that few of them would wish), to enter into contracts and experience their autonomy to the full extent that men enjoyed. But, despite the fact that the political/legal system has in the past privileged the few, has contemporary civil rights and affirmative action legislation not taken care of the problem?

Linda Gordon's discussion of state response to family violence is helpful in examining state intervention:

> women's historians represent social control as half of a bargain in which material benefits—welfare benefits, for example—are given to those controlled in exchange for the surrender of power or autonomy.[37]

What then can be said of women's lack of autonomy: that they reject autonomy as a primary value in their lives? Nancy Fraser and Linda Nicholson "pull us back from the brink" that essentialist arguments lead us to:

> Since the late 1970's, feminist social theorists have largely ceased speaking of biological determinants or a cross-cultural domestic/public separation. Many, moreover, have given up the assumption of monocausality. Nevertheless, some feminist social theorists have continued implicitly to suppose a quasi-metanarrative conception of theory. They have continued to theorize in terms of a putatively unitary, primary, culturally universal type of activity associated with women, generally an activity conceived as domestic and located in the family.[38]

But, their argument leaves us in an uncomfortably attenuated position. For them, feminist political practice is a matter of alliances:

> It [feminist political practice] recognizes that the diversity of women's needs and experiences means that no single solution, on issues like child care, social security, and housing, can be adequate for all. Thus, the underlying premise of this practice is that, while some women share some common interests and face some common enemies, such commonalities are by no means universal; rather, they are interlaced with differences, even conflicts.[39]

As they are located, women require both negative and positive rights to protect their welfare and their autonomy. Yet, as I argue in chapter 1, civil legislation, conceived as a *positive* intervention to assure certain access for women (and minorities), constitutes only protections against public restrictions, that is, *negative* freedoms. Such legislation fails to take into account (1) the power of the social and cultural construction of "woman" and (2) the fact that civil legislation may be rescinded and its provisions may be withdrawn by the state. It is, therefore, the remnants of women's traditional location that continue to require assessment.

Distribution of Labor

In the foregoing sections, I have argued that the construction of women's position and the ascription of their roles have made it possible to identify them as ostensibly protected from government "interference." They have also been "protected" from self-sufficiency and autonomy. The valuative distance between uncompensated work done in private and compensated work done in public has been exaggerated by the systemic focus on property. This valuative distinction has had a profound effect on the perception of women's contribution to economic stability within the state. Not only does this devaluation of women's contributions affect the perception of them as citizens, disregard of their contributions has sustained their very particular status as adjunct to male family members. Despite this exclusionary practice, women were not considered an oppressed category because women were not a category to be considered at all. This argument is well-documented and serves here only to provide a reminder of the basic differences in the white, propertied male experience of liberal democracy and the experiences of others, particularly women.

Are the delineations that were created to protect the citizenry from state intervention in wholly private matters unambiguous goods for all who experience the distinctions between public and private? Or is the foundation and development of liberalism antithetical to the welfare and equal treatment of some of those whom it is purported to protect? Catharine MacKinnon very clearly thinks that it is:

> Our social *treatment* certainly is different—the difference between power and powerlessness. Woman's commonality, which includes our diversity, comes from our shared social position. This is our explanation of our situation. I want to know: does Mrs. Schlafly think rape, battery, prostitution, incest, sexual harassment, unequal pay, and forced maternity express, to use her phrase, "the differences reasonable people wish to make" between women and men?[40]

Yet, is access to positive rights the ultimate answer? Robin West, in *Narrative, Authority, and Law,* proposes that:

> We address the multiple problems posed by our differences from men by adopting a critical method that aims directly for women's subjective well-being, rather than indirectly through a gauze of definitional presuppositions about the nature of human life that almost invariably exclude women's lives.[41]

Both MacKinnon and West seem to advocate a fundamental reworking of the privileged position of an individualist rights discourse in our legal and political theories. Rather than continuing to attempt to make women fit the preexisting model of atomistic-individual-as-rights-holder, contemporary theorists have begun to question the models themselves. The persistence of these attitudes can be attributed to the limited definition of autonomy that prevails in the United States, especially as autonomy is associated with individualism.

Individualism

The foundation of liberalism and the nucleus around which all boundaries are drawn is the individual. Individualism within the liberal state denies the ultimate power of the state and is contingent, as a fundamental prerequisite, on equality for all. Yet, the coincidence of patriarchal tradition, individualism, democracy, and a market economy, as they are uniquely interactive within the United States, engenders very particular dynamics within the socioeconomic and political structures. These dynamics and their interaction, in turn, (1) dictate private and familial relationships and (2) bind citizens to specific ideas as to the proper distribution of labor and the equitable ascription of roles. Finally, the operation of these dynamics has dictated who actually gets to ascribe roles, who defines and allocates rights, and who is qualified to decide which sets of values are immutable. Thus, individualism, as it is described by the American experience, has its unique character (primarily) by virtue of the form that it takes despite a historically amalgamous culture. The following analysis of different aspects of individualism assumes the intersection of these various components of the uniquely American system.

Possessive Individualism

Though inhabitants of Locke's precivil society negotiated contentious issues based on reason and fairness, there were, nevertheless, "inconveniences." The inconveniences of this relatively unenforceable social organization within the state of nature were ostensibly alleviated by the creation of a civil structure that operated only by the consent of the people. All those who agreed to have their public relationships administered by the structure were considered full citizens. However, the Lockean civil society, in practice, did not require for its operation the "consent" of any but propertied males. In fact, the primary purpose of the civil structure was protection of property—property in oneself and acquired property. Thus, the Lockean model of civil society was premised upon the inextricable connection between politics and economics. Given the Lockean definition of a full citizen, laws were established to protect, and have served to sustain, unequal wealth.[42] Civil society clearly privileged the propertied male and outlined a patently unfair, yet "just"—in the legal sense of the word "justified"—system.[43]

Lockean civil society, thus, embodied distinctions that clearly presaged a class system. According to MacPherson,[44] liberal democratic theory in the twentieth century very consciously sustains class distinctions. Though the Lockean emphasis on property was challenged early on and was not universally accepted as the optimal basis for American civil and legal systems,[45] it succeeded primarily because it served well those who were involved in the process of creating these systems. "Others"—those not considered full citizens within the systemic structure—were marginalized by virtue of their lack of real property, their race, or their gender.[46]

Yet, even as the privileged were forced to recognize that some "others" were not served by the classist, racist biases of the system, women were still not recognized as a marginalized group. MacPherson explains, very succinctly, the phenomenon of women's exclusion from the category of "excluded": "women were not included in the category of the marginalized because they did not constitute a class."[47] Women were not propertied; they were, themselves, property.

Rugged Individualism

The psychological form that individualism has taken is termed "rugged individualism." As a motivating concept it remains alive and well in the United States:

> The idea that a state should take action to affirm equality of opportunity was replaced by a classic notion of rugged individualism. . . . [t]his individualism was positioned against established civil rights discourse in order to discredit that discourse as well as feminist demands. Such legislation was earmarked as discriminatory in reverse.[48]

This perception of the ideal self has served to turn the responsibility for exclusion onto the excluded. Rugged individualism has come to represent the ideal model of a "true American." The hyperimage of independence and self-sufficiency that emerges from this model is reinforced by notions of the "pioneering spirit" of early settlers, and the revolutionary foundation of the state. Despite the fact that it has no basis in reality, Americans' romance with the concept of an ideal self and the shame that haunts the—inevitably—less than ideal self, has resulted in considerable inflexibility within the system, an inflexibility that circumscribes legitimate state provisions for, and restrictions upon, its citizens. It is therefore not surprising that the prevailing work ethic dictates that one (ostensibly) prospers by one's own wit and wisdom, and, above all, hard (paid) labor.

Realization of the American Dream is contingent upon experiencing a carefully proscribed and particular form of autonomy.[49] The American hyperimage derives primarily from the idea of the atomistic individual as the epitome of self-sustenance: the understanding that one survives—even thrives (and by implication, fails) by one's own hand—in isolation and without excuse. Inherent in that understanding is the belief that those who do not thrive are somehow flawed or unworthy—hence, not endowed with the proper capacity to be full citizens. This perception serves to legitimize conditions that reinforce a type of social Darwinism: the "survival of the fittest" in the absence of significant regard as to whether the fittest are "fitted out" by a previous generation, whether they struggle valiantly against their beginnings to no avail, or whether the workings of the market hold no particular sway in their lives.

Clearly, Americans within a liberal democracy face a dilemma that members of authoritarian or totalitarian regimes do not. The freedoms and protections that Americans enjoy—those that make public debate over contentious issues possible—are not available in these other states. Yet, the pervasive lethargy concerning existing conditions and paranoia around what "change"[50] might mean is as inhibiting as any totalitarian regime could hope to be.[51] The same freedoms and protections that make debate possible seem to assure us that having arrived at these particular social, legal, and political systems "freely" their institution must be natural and correct.

Autonomy

It is reasonable to assume that, in the absence of a liberal system of government, respect for the moral priority of the individual would not necessarily exist. It is also reasonable to assume that the priority of the individual should entail a significant amount of autonomy. Yet, theories of individualism guaranteed by the liberal state are quite varied in relation to the amount and quality of autonomy experienced by "unlike" members of the state. Within this culture, autonomy is understood as a function of a citizen's uninhibited operation over time within particular public/political settings, and the citizen's resulting sense of completeness. Citizens are *intellectually* autonomous having freely (to the extent that any person is truly "free") chosen, if not the system's direct effect on themselves, at least the basic tenets of the system given they have the capacity, education, and other cognitive wherewithal to make the appropriate choices for themselves.[52] It follows that human beings are *politically* autonomous given the state's structural capacity to recognize them as full and active participants in the public discourse. Quite simply, the politically autonomous are constitutionally[53] capable of entering and affecting the public/political system. Beyond recognition by the state, the individual is *psychologically* autonomous given the societal and developmental impetus to avail herself of the rights and freedoms she is afforded in the public space. The interaction and complementarity of these separate forces in the life of an individual citizen affects the perceptions of others, self-perception, and often actual capacity and/or energy around certain capabilities.[54] These dimensions of autonomy, therefore, play an integral role in the realization of equity within the system. However, before advancing an argument for greater autonomy for women, it is necessary to clearly delineate the parameters of the concept.

Individualism and autonomy have constituted complementary (sometimes indistinguishable) characteristics within the liberal tradition. Yet, this complementarity has been denied full growth and development in particular lives as a result of traditional societal precepts. The requisite characteristics for full membership are embodied by only a few individuals within the carefully circumscribed limits of state responsibility. Autonomy, as it is understood in this culture, implies radical independence from others and is, by definition, limited to those who are free to experience cognitively, psychologically and politically the objective capacity to influence the public decisions that directly affect their lives.

As they are socially defined, women are not individuals; women continue to be defined by their connections and their embeddedness in the private space. They are not recognized as cognitively, nor are they psychologically, "objective."[55] Objectivity has traditionally been recognized as a uniquely masculine capacity. Any success that a woman has in the public areas of life is commensurate with her ability to deny the ways that she differs from the male model. All this despite the fact that to the extent that the U.S. system operates under an assumption of the validity of this model, it has also served to limit the autonomous male's experience of connectedness.

The argument that this perception is an integral part of our history is made quite convincingly by Christine Sylvester when she argues that "masculine reactive autonomy" is played out in liberal political theory as stories about radically independent, self-generated beings entering into contracts unencumbered by relational attachments.[56] Thus, the definition of autonomy is laden with cultural and historical prejudice. The restricted sense of autonomy that these prejudices engender does not describe women's experience nor should women want to don that straitjacket to achieve parity. It is therefore necessary to recognize alternative forms of autonomy that describe the actual experience of human intersubjectivity, that is, a dynamic autonomy that has divested itself of the rigidity demanded by narrow, historical constructs. As Evelyn Fox Keller makes clear,

> a dynamic conception of autonomy leaves unchallenged a "potential space" between self and other—the "neutral area of experience" that, as D. W. Winnicott describes it, allows the temporary suspension of boundaries between "me" and "not-me" required for all empathic experience—experience that allows for the creative leap between knower and known. It acknowledges the ebb and flow between subject and object as the prerequisite for both love and knowledge.[57]

Keller argues that human nature requires a tension, not opposition, between autonomy and intimacy, separation and connection, aggression and love.

She believes that power can be reconceived in terms of mutuality and well-being rather than in terms of conflict and domination.

Susan James makes a similar argument in that:

> Emotional dependence is, after all primarily presented as a private virtue, firmly rooted in the domestic, female, apolitical institutions of society, where it is reflected in all sorts of practices and habits of thought. Cultural feminism suggests that analogues of these attitudes and practices could be extended beyond the bounds of what is currently regarded as the private sphere and incorporated into a new kind of politics—situated, sensitive to difference and caring.[58]

James, like Keller, emphasizes the tension rather than the supposed opposition between dependence and objectivity. What is renounced by her argument is the still prevalent tendency, even among feminists, to delegitimize those things that are of women; to deny the need to incorporate women's ways of knowing into the public discourse. Disclaiming association with those understandings is in effect a defense against rejection. Further, it is an attempt to fit the artificial construct that we have, as a society, created for men.

In the two hundred years of its existence, the United States has made significant inroads in the protection of women's rights.[59] This progress, nevertheless, says as much about the tenacity of women as it does about the corrigibility of the system. If the claims that liberalism makes are to be realized by every citizen, there must be some acknowledgment of the fact that, despite its express restriction of governance to the public sphere of life, the government of a liberal democracy within a market economy, such as exists in the United States, profoundly intervenes and regulates the private lives of citizens in numerous, though possibly tacit ways.[60]

State action to eradicate institutions of oppression becomes imperative when, as a result of social and institutional structures, the individual does not experience (intellectually, psychologically, or politically) the autonomy to avail herself of practical opportunities.[61] Women's contributions are critical to the continued existence and development of the state. Therefore, the "invisibilization" of women's productive and reproductive efforts is a denial of the integral nature of their labor in the operation and continuation of the system. Denying them equal opportunity and access to political processes, health care, education, and compensation for their labor on an equal level with men is debilitating to contemporary family structures and, ultimately, to the state. Alternatively, recognition of dynamic autonomy within a just system based on the narratives of lived experience constitutes a state in which women (and men) may experience well-being and mutuality.

Legal Rights of Men and Women

As a direct result of the aforementioned conditions, the liberal legal system in the United States has developed in the absence of real definitions of the harms that women suffer. Because the definitions and assumptions are not simply legally, but also culturally, determined and theologically reinforced, the definitions are more assiduously engrained in the social structure than simple reference to the development of case law would imply. It is predominantly the customary, not the legally proscribed, treatment of women that effectively denies their rightful status. Nonetheless, it is necessary to interrogate the U.S. legal system concerning its effect on women. How does one critique the U.S. legal system? Robin West argues that it is precisely the empathic recognition of self in other that is necessary to afford primacy to the "ought to be" rather than the "is" in adjudication. She makes the argument that it is the effect of the act that must be criticized

> An act of power in public life as well as in private life that is praiseworthy is an act of power that, in short, is loving: it is the act that originates in the heart and is prompted by our sympathy for the needs of others, and empathy for their situation. I see no reason not to hold adjudicatory acts of power to this standard. . . . Indeed, the strength of the opinion lies more in its willingness to ignore the community's texts rather than its willingness to read them: the opinion speaks to our real need for fraternity rather than our expressed xenophobia; and it taps our real potential for an enlarged community and an enlarged conception of self rather than our expressed fear of differences.[62]

At this point in our history women should be fully aware that their rights are not protected in the liberal legal system in exactly the way that the legal rights of men have been protected. The structure of the legal system is such that the "agents" identified are exclusively white, propertied male—unless otherwise stated. It is therefore not simply the fundamental basis of liberalism that is problematic, but its very specific definition and development within the U.S. legal system.

Traditionally, the boundaries of the private realm were penetrated, at will, only by the franchised, autonomous male. What happens to those who, according to the system, never leave the private space? The fundamental question here is the effect of the liberal legal system on women relative to their male counterparts. The perception has been that women are protected—are beyond the mundane workings of the system—primarily because of their unique status as mother and caregiver. The individualism that characterizes the citizen does not describe women. They are, according to the roles ascribed them, inevitably attached—not individual. Women, as a result, have (at best) experienced minimal autonomy in the system as it was conceived.

Because case law and interpretations of the Constitution grew out of certain perceptions and expectations of the world, as the world changes these perceptions and expectations make considerably less sense. The challenge is to modify the legal structure in order to accommodate actual lived experience. But to what extent is it reasonable to alter the legal structure to accommodate social practices? To what extent should an attempt be made to salvage the basic structure of the law while addressing the ever-increasing concerns of those who are coming to recognize the inequity of the system in terms of their own identities and rights? How is it possible to discuss the incorporation of positive rights as an augmentation of—rather than as opposed to—negative rights in a primarily liberal system? How does one address the dilemma facing women: the negative right to privacy (that is, against forced maternity) versus positive intervention by the state in protection of women against spousal rape, for example?

Conclusion

The United States has not lived up to the claims of liberalism. Civil rights cannot remedy the failure of the state to recognize and respect its citizens' human rights. State-conferred civil rights constitute an insufficient remedy to human rights violations. Human rights are not legitimately conferred or denied by the state. As argued in chapter 1, civil legislation finds its appropriate expression only in the presence of a higher standard; a standard that denies the state authority beyond its administration of the will of its citizens because they are human. Yet, liberal democracy in the United States was founded upon a white, male standard that denied women's full citizenship. If citizens are human and therefore have inherent human rights, women's exclusion from full citizenship meant, perforce, that the state was flawed at its inception in its (functional) definition of humanity. State-conferred civil rights fail to reclaim the virtues of liberalism especially and most importantly in the face of enduring attitudes that these rights abridge the fundamental individualist conceptions of citizenship. The pervasive attitude is that they offer "special" consideration to the few, thus discriminating against the (white, heterosexual, propertied male) citizen who meets all the criteria of citizenship without recourse to undue state intervention. This attitude is reinforced by certain legislative protections. Women have struggled *against* the imposition of "protective" legislation that infantilizes them. They cannot afford to be satisfied with the "corrective" legislation that essentially obscures fundamental systemic problems. Women must struggle for "emancipatory" provisions that enumerate and specifically address the particular harms that they suffer. As I argued in chapter 2, past legislation and the tendency of judges to rely upon and preserve traditional understandings has resulted in judicial interpretations that disregard the actual differences between men and women.

I have argued that the construction of women's position and the ascription of their roles have made it possible to identify them as ostensibly protected from government "interference." They have also been "protected" from self-sufficiency and autonomy. The primary focus on acquisition—the economic dimension of the public arena—has served to exaggerate the valuative distance between uncompensated work done in private and compensated work done in public. This valuative distinction has had a profound effect on the perception of women's contributions to economic stability within the state. Not only does this devaluation of women's contributions affect the perception of them as citizens, disregard of their contributions has sustained their very particular status as adjunct to male family members. Despite these exclusionary practices, women are not considered an oppressed category because women are not a category to be considered at all. Women who have experienced some measure of success in the public realm do so primarily in direct proportion to their willingness and capacity to adopt the male model.

The attempts that the United States has made over the years to correct its treatment of women and minorities are laudatory. Those efforts notwithstanding, the "idea" of human rights supercedes and displaces the "idea" of civil rights. My argument is not that women will immediately and fully experience the full measure of equity through ratification of CEDAW. The struggle that women face, nationally and internationally, is to gain access to remedies that respond directly to their harms, not simply equal to those of their male counterparts.[63] The idea that women should be "equal" to men has become increasingly problematic, as the epigraph to this chapter expresses quite persuasively.

Ratification of CEDAW is an opportunity to claim the fundamental, ideological premises of liberalism for women. Each article of CEDAW functions very particularly and practically to rectify the marginalizing effects of the system and to alleviate women's oppression.[64] Moreover, CEDAW carefully outlines both general and specific remedies for the systemic inequities and oppressive societal biases that have limited women's participation and equal operation within the state. The actual structure of the convention[65] describes a necessary and specific movement from very abstract and generally accepted premises into the depths of the "dark corners" of women's lived experiences. The experiences of women have been invisibilized by traditional cultural and social constructs, political norms and legal standards in virtually every nation of the world. Thus, the strictures of the convention force an interrogation of traditional norms and standards, and require each state party to assume an active role in eliminating the gender-based inequitable treatment of its citizens.

Whether the United States could serve as a model in globalizing concern for women's human rights remains to be seen. As changes have occurred and an increasing number of women have become heads-of-households, the legal system that manifestly ignores their existence has been recognized as inadequate.[66] Nevertheless, there is continued resistance to rectifying women's unequal status and that resistance is based on the argument that maintenance of their traditional roles is integral to (1) the economic stability of the state; (2) the emotional, psychological, and nutritional health of children; (3) the education and socialization of children; and (4) the maintenance of the family (as the principle organ of social order). Therefore, incorporation of women's human rights, and the subsequent alteration of the conditions of their oppression, would seem to pose a fundamental threat to the stability of the state, the welfare of its children, and the privacy afforded the nuclear family. Yet, if commitment to liberal ideals is a primary goal of the state, then adherence to the basic precepts of liberalism is a requirement for the realization of that goal. Given this premise, the welfare of the world and its people is dependent upon the inclusion and free expression of all citizens as full participants in the institutions and organs that have a profound affect on their lives. Universal ratification of CEDAW without substantive reservations is a necessary step toward inclusion of women, as full citizens, in that participation.

Appendix 🪷

The International Convention On Elimination of All Forms of Discrimination against Women

The States Parties to the present Convention,

Noting that the Charter of the United Nations reaffirms faith in fundamental human rights, in the dignity and worth of the human person and in the equal rights of men and women,

Noting that the Universal Declaration of Human Rights affirms the principle of the inadmissibility of discrimination and proclaims that all human beings are born free and equal in dignity and rights and that everyone is entitled to all the rights and freedoms set forth therein, without distinction of any kind, including distinction based on sex,

Noting that the States Parties to the International Covenants on Human Rights have the obligation to ensure the equal right of men and women to enjoy all economic, social, cultural, civil and political rights,

Considering the international conventions concluded under the auspices of the United Nations and the specialized agencies promoting equality of rights of men and women,

Noting also the resolutions, declarations and recommendations adopted by the United Nations and the specialized agencies promoting equality of rights of men and women,

Concerned, however, that despite these various instruments extensive discrimination against women continues to exist,

Recalling that discrimination against women violates the principles of equality of rights and respect for human dignity, is an obstacle to the participation of women, on equal terms with men, in the political, social, economic and cultural life of their countries, hampers the growth of the prosperity of society and the family and makes more difficult the full development of the potentialities of women in the service of their countries and of humanity,

Concerned that in situations of poverty women have the least access to food, health, education, training and opportunities for employment and other needs,

Convinced that the establishment of the new international economic order based on equity and justice will contribute significantly towards the promotion of equality between men and women,

Emphasizing that the eradication of apartheid, of all forms of racism, racial discrimination, colonialism, neocolonialism, aggression, foreign occupation and domination and interference in the internal affairs of States is essential to the full enjoyment of the rights of men and women,

Affirming that the strengthening of international peace and security, relaxation of international tension, mutual co-operation among all States irrespective of their social and economic systems, general and complete disarmament, and in particular nuclear disarmament under strict and effective international control, the affirmation of the principles of justice, equality and mutual benefit in relations among countries and the realization of the right of peoples under alien and colonial domination and foreign occupation to self-determination and independence, as well as respect for national sovereignty and territorial integrity, will promote social progress and development and as a consequence will contribute to the attainment of full equality between men and women,

Convinced that the full and complete development of a country, the welfare of the world and the cause of peace require the maximum participation of women on equal terms with men in all fields,

Bearing in mind the great contribution of women to the welfare of the family and to the development of society, so far not fully recognized, the social significance of maternity and the role of both parents in the family and in the upbringing of children, and aware that the role of women in procreation should not be a basis for discrimination but that the upbringing of children requires a sharing of responsibility between men and women and society as a whole,

Aware that a change in the traditional role of men as well as the role of women in society and in the family is needed to achieve full equality between men and women,

Determined to implement the principles set forth in the Declaration on the Elimination of Discrimination against Women and, for that purpose, to adopt the measures required for the elimination of such discrimination in all its forms and manifestations,

Have agreed on the following:

Part I

Article 1

For the purposes of the present Convention, the term "discrimination against women" shall mean any distinction, exclusion or restriction mode on the basis of sex which has the effect or purpose of impairing or nullifying the recognition, enjoyment or exercise by women, irrespective of their marital status, on a basis of equality of men and women, of human rights and fundamental freedoms in the political, economic, social, cultural, civil or any other field.

Article 2

States Parties condemn discrimination against women in all its forms, agree to pursue by all appropriate means and without delay a policy of eliminating discrimination against women and, to this end, undertake:

a. To embody the principle of the equality of men and women in their notional constitutions or other appropriate legislation if not yet incorporated therein and to ensure, through law and other appropriate means, the practical realization of this principle;
b. To adopt appropriate legislative and other measures, including sanctions where appropriate, prohibiting all discrimination against women;
c. To establish legal protection of the rights of women on an equal basis with men and to ensure through competent national tribunals and other public institutions the effective protection of women against any act of discrimination;
d. To refrain from engaging in any act or practice of discrimination against women and to ensure that public authorities and institutions shall act in conformity with this obligation;
e. To take all appropriate measures to eliminate discrimination against women by any person, organization or enterprise;
f. To take all appropriate measures, including legislation, to modify or abolish existing laws, regulations, customs and practices which constitute discrimination against women;
g. To repeal all national penal provisions which constitute discrimination against women.

Article 3

States Parties shall take in all fields, in particular in the political, social, economic and cultural fields, all appropriate measures, including legislation, to ensure the full development and advancement of women, for the purpose of guaranteeing them the exercise and enjoyment of human rights and fundamental freedoms on a basis of equality with men.

Article 4

1. Adoption by States Parties of temporary special measures aimed at accelerating de facto equality between men and women shall not be considered discrimination as defined in the present Convention, but shall in no way entail as a consequence the maintenance of unequal or separate standards; these measures shall be discontinued when the objectives of equality of opportunity and treatment have been achieved.
2. Adoption by States Parties of special measures, including those measures contained in the present Convention, aimed at protecting maternity shall not be considered discriminatory.

Article 5

States Parties shall take all appropriate measures:

a. To modify the social and cultural patterns of conduct of men and women, with a view to achieving the elimination of prejudices and customary and all other practices which are based on the idea of the inferiority or the superiority of either of the sexes or on stereotyped roles for men and women;
b. To ensure that family education includes a proper understanding of maternity as a social function and the recognition of the common responsibility of men and women in the upbringing and development of their children, it being understood that the interest of the children is the primordial consideration in all cases.

Article 6

States Parties shall take all appropriate measures, including legislation, to suppress all forms of traffic in women and exploitation of prostitution of women.

Part II

Article 7

States Parties shall take all appropriate measures to eliminate discrimination against women in the political and public life of the country and, in particular, shall ensure to women, on equal terms with men, the right:

a. To vote in all elections and public referenda and to be eligible for election to all publicly elected bodies;
b. To participate in the formulation of government policy and the implementation thereof and to hold public office and perform all public functions at all levels of government;
c. To participate in non-governmental organizations and associations concerned with the public and political life of the country.

Article 8

States Parties shall take all appropriate measures to ensure to women, on equal terms with men and without any discrimination, the opportunity to represent their Governments at the international level and to participate in the work of international organizations.

Article 9

1. States Parties shall grant women equal rights with men to acquire, change or retain their nationality. They shall ensure in particular that neither marriage

to an alien nor change of nationality by the husband during marriage shall automatically change the nationality of the wife, render her stateless or force upon her the nationality of the husband.

2. States Parties shall grant women equal rights with men with respect to the nationality of their children.

Part III

Article 10

States Parties shall take all appropriate measures to eliminate discrimination against women in order to ensure to them equal rights with men in the field of education and in particular to ensure, on a basis of equality of men and women:

a. The same conditions for career and vocational guidance, for access to studies and for the achievement of diplomas in educational establishments of all categories in rural as well as in urban areas; this equality shall be ensured in preschool, general, technical, professional and higher technical education, as well as in all types of vocational training;

b. Access to the same curricula, the same examinations, teaching staff with qualifications of the same standard and school premises and equipment of the same quality;

c. The elimination of any stereotyped concept of the roles of men and women at all levels and in all forms of education by encouraging coeducation and other types of education which will help to achieve this aim and, in particular, by the revision of textbooks and school programs and the adaptation of teaching methods;

d. The same opportunities to benefit from scholarships and other study grants;

e. The same opportunities for access to programmes of continuing education, including adult and functional literacy programmes, particularly those aimed at reducing, at the earliest possible time, any gap in education existing between men and women;

f. The reduction of female student drop-out rates and the organization of programmes for girls and women who have left school prematurely;

g. The same opportunities to participate actively in sports and physical education;

h. Access to specific educational information to help to ensure the health and well-being of families, including information and advice on family planning.

Article 11

1. States Parties shall take all appropriate measures to eliminate discrimination against women in the field of employment in order to ensure, on a basis of equality of men and women, the same rights, in particular:

   a. The right to work as an inalienable right of all human beings;

b. The right to the same employment opportunities, including the application of the same criteria for selection in matters of employment;

c. The right to free choice of profession and employment, the right to promotion, job security and all benefits and conditions of service and the right to receive vocational training and retraining, including apprenticeships, advanced vocational training and recurrent training;

d. The right to equal renumeration, including benefits, and to equal treatment in respect of work of equal value, as well as equality of treatment in the evaluation of the quality of work;

e. The right to social security, particularly in cases of retirement, unemployment, sickness, invalidity and old age and other incapacity to work, as well as the right to paid leave;

f. The right to protection of health and to safety in working conditions, including the safeguarding of the function of reproduction.

2. In order to prevent discrimination against women on the grounds of marriage or maternity and to ensure their effective right to work, States Parties shall take appropriate measures:

a. To prohibit, subject to the imposition of sanctions, dismissal on the grounds of pregnancy or of maternity leave and discrimination in dismissals on the basis of marital status;

b. To introduce maternity leave with pay or with comparable social benefits without loss of former employment, seniority or social allowances;

c. To encourage the provision of the necessary supporting social services to enable parents to combine family obligations with work responsibilities and participation in public life, in particular through promoting the establishment and development of a network of child-care facilities;

d. To provide special protection to women during pregnancy in types of work proved to be harmful to them.

3. Protective legislation relating to matters covered in this article shall be reviewed periodically in the light of scientific and technological knowledge and shall be revised, repealed or extended as necessary.

Article 12

1. States Parties shall take all appropriate measures to eliminate discrimination against women in the field of health care in order to ensure, on a basis of equality of men and women, access to health care services, including those related to family planning.

2. Notwithstanding the provisions of paragraph 1 of this article, States Parties shall ensure to women appropriate services in connection with pregnancy, confinement and the post-natal period, granting free services where necessary, as well as adequate nutrition during pregnancy and lactation.

Article 13

1. States Parties shall take all appropriate measures to eliminate discrimination against women in other areas of economic and social life in order to ensure, on a basis of equality of men and women, the some rights, in particular:

   a. The right to family benefits;
   b. The right to bank loans, mortgages and other forms of financial credit;
   c. The right to participate in recreational activities, sports and all aspects of cultural life.

Article 14

1. States Parties shall take into account the particular problems faced by rural women and the significant roles which rural women play in the economic survival of their families, including their work in the non-monetized sectors of the economy, and shall take all appropriate measures to ensure the application of the provisions of this Convention to women in rural areas.
2. States Parties shall take all appropriate measures to eliminate discrimination against women in rural areas in order to ensure, on a basis of equality of men and women, that they participate in and benefit from rural development and, in particular, shall ensure to such women the right:

   a. To participate in the elaboration and implementation of development planning at all levels;
   b. To have access to adequate health care facilities, including information, counseling and services in family planning;
   c. To benefit directly from social security programmes;
   d. To obtain all types of training and education, formal and non-formal, including that relating to functional literacy, as well as, inter alia, the benefit of all community and extension services, in order to increase their technical proficiency;
   e. To organize self-help groups and co-operatives in order to obtain equal access to economic opportunities through employment or self-employment;
   f. To participate in all community activities;
   g. To have access to agricultural credit and loans, marketing facilities, appropriate technology and equal treatment in land and agrarian reform as well as in land resettlement schemes;
   h. To enjoy adequate living conditions, particularly in relation to housing, sanitation, electricity and water supply, transport and communications.

Part IV

Article 15

1. States Parties shall accord to women equality with men before the law.

2. States Parties shall accord to women, in civil matters, a legal capacity identical to that of men and the same opportunities to exercise that capacity. In particular, they shall give women equal rights to conclude contracts and to administer property and shall treat them equally in all stages of procedure in courts and tribunals.

3. States Parties agree that all contracts and all other private instruments of any kind with a legal effect which is directed at restricting the legal capacity of women shall be deemed null and void.

4. States Parties shall accord to men and women the same rights with regard to the law relating to the movement of persons and the freedom to choose their residence and domicile.

Article 16

1. States Parties shall take all appropriate measures to eliminate discrimination against women in all matters relating to marriage and family relations and in particular shall ensure, on a basis of equality of men and women:

    a. The same right to enter into marriage;
    b. The same right freely to choose spouse and to enter into marriage only with their free and full consent;
    c. The same rights and responsibilities during marriage and at its dissolution;
    d. The same rights and responsibilities as parents, irrespective of their marital status, in matters relating to their children; in all cases the interests of the children shall be paramount;
    e. The same rights to decide freely and responsibly on the number and spacing of their children and to have access to the information, education and means to enable them to exercise these rights,
    f. The same rights and responsibilities with regard to guardianship, wardship, trusteeship and adoption of children, or similar institutions where these concepts exist in national legislation; in all cases the interests of the children shall be paramount;
    g. The same personal rights as husband and wife, including the right to choosing a family name, a profession and an occupation;
    h. The same rights for both spouses in respect of the ownership, acquisition, management, administration, enjoyment and disposition of property, whether free of charge or for a valuable consideration.

2. The betrothal and the marriage of a child shall have no legal effect, and all necessary action, including legislation, shall be taken to specify a minimum age for marriage and to make the registration of marriages in an official registry compulsory.

Part V

Article 17

1. For the purpose of considering the progress made in the implementation of the present Convention, there shall be established a Committee on the Elimination of Discrimination against Women (hereinafter referred to as the Committee) consisting, at the time of entry into force of the Convention, of eighteen and, after ratification of or accession to the Convention by the thirty-fifth State Party, of twenty-three experts of high moral standing and competence in the field covered by the Convention. The experts shall be elected by States Parties from among their nationals and shall serve in their personal capacity, consideration being given to equitable geographical distribution and to the representation of the different forms of civilization as well as the principle legal systems.

2. The members of the Committee shall be elected by secret ballot from a list of persons nominated by States Parties. Each State Party may nominate one person from among its own nationals.

3. The initial election shall be held six months after the date of the entry into force of the present Convention. At least three months before the date of each election the Secretary-General of the United Nations shall address a letter to the States Parties inviting them to submit their nominations within two months. The Secretary-General shall prepare a list in alphabetical order of all persons thus nominated, indicating the States Parties which have nominated them, and shall submit it to the States Parties.

4. Elections of the members of the Committee shall be held at a meeting of States Parties convened by the Secretary-General at United Nations Headquarters. At that meeting, for which two-thirds of the States Parties shall constitute a quorum, the persons elected to the Committee shall be those nominees who obtain the largest number of votes and an absolute majority of the votes of the representatives of States Parties present and voting.

5. The members of the Committee shall be elected for a term of four years. However, the terms of nine of the members elected at the first election shall expire at the end of two years; immediately after the first election the names of these nine members shall be chosen by lot by the Chairman of the Committee.

6. The election of the five additional members of the Committee shall be held in accordance with the provisions of paragraphs 2, 3, and 4 of this article, following the thirty-fifth ratification or accession. The terms of two of the additional members elected on this occasion shall expire at the end of two years, the names of these two members having been chosen by lot by the Chairman of the Committee.

7. For the filling of casual vacancies, the State Party whose expert has ceased to function as a member of the Committee shall appoint another expert from among its nationals, subject to the approval of the Committee.

8. The members of the Committee shall, with the approval of the General Assembly, receive emoluments from United Nations resources on such terms and conditions as the Assembly may decide, having regard to the importance of the Committee's responsibilities.

9. The Secretary-General of the United Nations shall provide the necessary staff and facilities for the effective performance of the functions of the Committee under the present Convention.

Article 18

1. States Parties undertake to submit to the Secretary-General of the United Nations, for consideration by the Committee, a report on the legislative, judicial, administrative or other measures which they have adopted to give effect to the provisions of the present Convention and on the progress made in this respect:

   a. Within a year after the entry into force for the State concerned; and
   b. Thereafter at least every four years and further whenever the Committee so requests.

2. Reports may indicate factors and difficulties affecting the degree of fulfillment of obligations under the present Convention.

Article 19

1. The Committee shall adopt its own rules of procedure.
2. The Committee shall elect its officers for a term of two years.

Article 20

1. The Committee shall normally meet for a period of not more than two weeks annually in order to consider the reports submitted in accordance with article 18 of the present Convention.
2. The meetings of the Committee shall normally be held at United Nations Headquarters or at any other convenient place as determined by the Committee.

Article 2l

1. The Committee shall, through the Economic and Social Council, report annually to the General Assembly of the United Nations on its activities and may make suggestions and general recommendations based on the examination of reports and information received from the States Parties. Such suggestions and general recommendations shall be included in the report of the Committee together with comments, if any, from States Parties.

2. The Secretary-General shall transmit the reports of the Committee to the Commission on the Status of Women for its information.

Article 22

The specialized agencies shall be entitled to be represented at the consideration of the implementation of such provisions of the present Convention as fall within the scope of their activities. The Committee may invite the specialized agencies to submit reports on the implementation of the Convention in areas falling within the scope of their activities.

Part VI

Article 23

Nothing in this Convention shall affect any provisions that are more conducive to the achievement of equality between men and women which may be contained:

a. In the legislation of a State Party; or
b. In any other international convention, treaty or agreement in force for that State.

Article 24

States Parties undertake to adopt all necessary measures at the national level aimed at achieving the full realization of the rights recognized in the present Convention.

Article 25

1. The present Convention shall be open for signature by all States.
2. The Secretary-General of the United Nations is designated as the depositary of the present Convention.
3. The present Convention is subject to ratification. Instruments of ratification shall be deposited with the Secretary-General of the United Nations.
4. The present Convention shall be open to accession by all States. Accession shall be effected by the deposit of an instrument of accession with the Secretary-General of the United Nations.

Article 26

1. A request for the revision of the present Convention may be made at any time by any State Party by means of a notification in writing addressed to the Secretary-General of the United Nations.
2. The General Assembly of the United Nations shall decide upon the steps, if any, to be taken in respect of such a request.

Article 27

1. The present Convention shall enter into force on the thirtieth day after the date of deposit with the Secretary-General of the United Nations of the twentieth instrument of ratification or accession.
2. For each State ratifying the present Convention or acceding to it after the deposit of the twentieth instrument of ratification or accession, the Convention shall enter into force on the thirtieth day after the date of the deposit of its own instrument of ratification or accession.

Article 28

1. The Secretary-General of the United Nations shall receive and circulate to all States the text of reservations made by States at the time of ratification or accession.
2. A reservation incompatible with the object and purpose of the present Convention shall not be permitted.
3. Reservations may be withdrawn at any time by notification to this effect addressed to the Secretary-General of the United Nations, who shall then inform all States thereof. Such notification shall take effect on the date on which it is received.

Article 29

1. Any dispute between two or more States Parties concerning the interpretation or application of the present Convention which is not settled by negotiation shall, at the request of one of them, be submitted to arbitration. If within six months from the date of the request for arbitration the parties are unable to agree on the organization of the arbitration, any one of those parties may refer the dispute to the International Court of Justice by request in conformity with the Statute of the Court.
2. Each State Party may at the time of signature or ratification of this Convention or accession thereto declare that it does not consider itself bound by paragraph 1 of this article. The other States Parties shall not be bound by that paragraph with respect to any State Party which has made such a reservation.
3. Any State Party that has made a reservation in accordance with paragraph 2 of this article may at any time withdraw that reservation by notification to the Secretary-General of the United Nations.

Article 30

The present Convention, the Arabic, Chinese, English, French, Russian and Spanish texts of which are equally authentic, shall be deposited with the Secretary-General of the United Nations.

Notes

Introduction

1. The Country Reports on Human Rights issued by the U.S. Department of State each year is the result of data gathered mostly by non-governmental organizations within the reporting countries.
2. For further discussion of the early perception of women's roles in development see particularly Hilkka Pietila and Jeanne Vickers, *Making Women Matter: the Role of the United Nations,* 3rd ed., London and New Jersey: Zed Books, 1994.
3. The Annual Human Rights Campaign of Amnesty International focused, in 1999, on human rights abuses in the United States. All of the named abuses came under the auspices of the Covenant on Civil and Political Rights. One reason: the United States has ratified the CCPR and could therefore legitimately be expected to adhere to its strictures. The second reason: Amnesty has traditionally focused exclusively on civil and political violations, so in following its own mandate investigates only those issues even though women's rights is of increasing concern.
4. On October 27, 1999, nine female House members were evicted from a hearing of the Senate Foreign Relations Committee when they attempted to present Committee Chairman Jesse Helms with a letter requesting hearings on the 1979 UN Convention to Eliminate All Forms of Discrimination against Women (CEDAW) treaty. Helms called the Capitol Police to take them out of the meeting. Helms is an opponent to the treaty and has refused to hold hearings on it, permit a vote, or even discuss it with House members who want ratification, despite the fact that the treaty has already been ratified by over 160 countries. For more details, see Helen Dewar, "'Ladies' of the House Rebuffed; Lawmakers Crash Senate Hearing; Helms Summons Police," *The Washington Post,* October 28, 1999, A31.
5. This sentiment is expressed quite well in Richard Rorty's text, *Achieving our Country,* Cambridge, MA: Harvard University Press, 1998
6. One might legitimately argue that the obstructions to ratification are key Senators who occupy critical positions within Congress, and to an extent that is correct. Nonetheless, the larger questions remain: Did they elect themselves? What of the twenty-odd years of non-ratification?

7. Dorothy McBride Stetson's text *Women's Rights in the U.S.A.: Policy Debates and Gender Roles,* Pacific Grove, CA: Brooks/Cole Publishing, 1991, is dedicated to explication of the realities for women in the contemporary United States.

8. The ongoing debate surrounding cultural relativism and universalism is particularly important to note here. Jack Donnelly provides a clear and comprehensive statement of the tensions inherent to the debate in his text, *International Human Rights,* 2nd ed., Boulder, CO: Westview Press, 1998. These issues are addressed more thoroughly in chapter 3.

Chapter 1

1. Angelina Grimke, "Human Rights Not Founded on Sex," in *Freedom, Feminism, and the State,* ed. Wendy McElroy (London: The Independent Institute, 1991), pp. 29–34.

2. Hilkka Pietila and Jeanne Vickers, *Making Women Matter: The Role of the United Nations* (London: Zed Books, 1990).

3. *Women, International Development, and Politics,* ed. Kathleen Staudt (Philadelphia: Temple University Press, 1990); *Women in the Face of Change: The Soviet Union, Eastern Europe, and China,* eds. Shirin Rai, Hilary Pilkington, and Annie Phizacklea (New York: Routledge, 1992); *Women Transforming Politics: Worldwide Strategies for Empowerment,* ed. Jill M. Bystydzienski (Bloomington: Indiana University Press, 1992).

4. Jack Donnelly, "Humanitarian Intervention and American Foreign Policy: Law, Morality, and Politics," in *Human Rights and the World Community: Issues and Action,* eds. Richard Pierre Claude and Burns H. Weston (Philadelphia: University of Pennsylvania Press, 1992).

5. James H. Cone, *Martin and Malcolm and America: A Dream or a Nightmare* (Maryknoll, NY: Orbis Books, 1993).

6. 488 U.S. 469 (1989), argued October 5, 1988, decided January 23, 1989.

7. Martha C. Nussbaum, "Human Functioning and Social Justice: In Defense of Aristotelian Essentialism," in *Political Theory,* vol.20, no. 2 (May 1992): 202–246.

8. Ibid., p. 227.

9. Dorothy McBride Stetson, *Women's Rights in the U.S.A.,* 2nd ed., New York: Garland Publishing, 1997, pp. 229–230.

10. Ibid., pp. 25–26.

11. John Gray, *Liberalism* (Minneapolis: University of Minnesota Press, 1995).

12. Barbara R. Bergmann, *In Defense of Affirmative Action* (New York: HarperCollins, 1996).

13. Dorothy McBride Stetson, *Women's Rights in the U.S.A.: Policy Debates and Gender Roles* (Pacific Grove, CA: Brooks/Cole, 1991).

14. Alice Kessler-Harris, "The Wage Conceived: Value and Need as Measures of a Woman's Worth," in *Feminist Frontiers IV,* eds. Laurel Richardson, Verta Taylor, Nancy Whittier (New York: The McGraw-Hill Companies, Inc., 1997), pp. 201–214.

15. Mary Ann Glendon, *Rights Talk: The Impoverishment of Political Discourse* (New York: The Free Press, 1991); Jane Flax, "Beyond Equality: Gender, Justice, and Difference," in *Beyond Equality and Difference: Citizenship, Feminist Politics, Female Subjectivity,* eds. Gisela Bock and Susan James (New York: Routledge, 1992), pp. 193–210.

16. Friedrich Neitzsche, *On the Advantages and Disadvantages of History for Life* (1874) trans. Peter Preuss (Cambridge: Hackett Publishing Company, Inc., 1980).

17. Celina Romany, "State Responsibility Goes Private: A Feminist Critique of the Public/Private Distinction in International Human Rights Law," in *Human Rights of Women: National and International Perspectives,* ed. Rebecca J. Cook (Philadelphia: University of Pennsylvania Press, 1994).

18. Belinda Clark, "The Vienna Convention Reservations Regime and the Convention On Discrimination against Women," in *The American Journal of International Law,* vol. 85 (1991): 282–283. In this article, Clark reports that as of December 31, 1980, one hundred states had ratified the Convention, of which forty-one had entered substantive reservations.

19. Louis Henkin, *The Age of Rights* (New York: Columbia University Press, 1990).

20. Johannes Morsink, "Women's Rights and the Universal Declaration," *Human Rights Quarterly,* vol.13, no. 2 (1991): 229–256.

21. Hilary Charlesworth, "What are 'Women's International Human Rights?'" *Human Rights of Women: National and International Perspectives,* ed. Rebecca J. Cook (Philadelphia: University of Pennsylvania Press, 1994).

22. Ibid.

23. Malcolm N. Shaw, *International Law* (Cambridge: Grotius Publications Limited, 1991).

24. Ibid., p. 194.

25. What follows is a short synopsis of the argument found in chapter 3.

26. Charlesworth, 1994.

27. Shaw, 1991, p. 188.

28. Bergmann, 1996.

29. Ibid., pp. 48–55.

30. Stetson, 1991.

31. Chapter 4 is a further investigation of U.S. unwillingness to extend its definition of human rights to more than civil and political rights. This unwillingness is reflected in U.S. failure to ratify the International Covenant on Economic, Social, and Cultural Rights, which virtually all human rights scholars see as indivisible from the International Covenant on Civil and Political Rights, which the United States has ratified.

32. Stetson, 1991.

Chapter 2

1. UN Treaty Series, vol. 1249, no. 20378, p. 13.

2. Celina Romany, "State Responsibility Goes Private: A Feminist Critique of the Public/Private Distinction in International Human Rights Law," in *Human Rights of Women: National and International Perspectives,* ed. Rebecca Cook (Philadelphia: University of Pennsylvania Press, 1994).

3. The Bricker Amendment has been cited as the defining document with regard to U.S. Senate attitudes toward ratification of international human rights treaties. For an excellent discussion of the debate, see Natalie Hevener Kaufman and David Whiteman, "Opposition to Human Rights Treaties in the United States Senate: The Legacy of the Bricker Amendment," *Human Rights Quarterly,* vol. 10, no. 3 (1988): 309–337. They write, "Our main conclusions are that proponents of the Bricker Amendment were primarily concerned with human rights treaties, that contemporary arguments against passage of human rights treaties have not changed substantially from arguments presented in the 1950's, and that the legacy of these earlier deliberations is still apparent in the attitude of those considering the treaties now."

4. For example, the United Nations Convention on the Prevention and Punishment of the Crime of Genocide was offered for ratification in 1951 and was not ratified by the United States until 1979.

5. *Basic Facts about the United Nations,* Department of Public Information (New York: United Nations, 1995), p. 189.

6. President Carter's transmittal of these treaties to Congress is discussed more thoroughly in chapter 4.

7. United States Senate Committee on Foreign Relations, *Convention on Elimination of All Forms of Discrimination against Women,* 101st Congr., 2nd Sess., August 2, 1990 (Washington, DC: Government Printing Office, 1991). United States House of Representatives Subcommittee on Human Rights and International Organizations, *International Human Rights Abuses Against Women,* 101st Congr., 2nd Sess., March 21 and July 26, 1990 (Washington, DC: Government Printing Office, 1991). Neither committee has since discussed human rights abuses against women (except to recognize abuses in China) or the possibility of CEDAW ratification.

8. This topic is covered at length in chapter 4.

9. Hilary Charlesworth, "What Are 'Women's International Human Rights'?" in *Human Rights of Women: National and International Perspectives,* ed. Rebecca J. Cook (Philadelphia: University of Pennsylvania Press, 1994), pp. 58–84.

10. Ibid.

11. For a thorough discussion of obstructions to recognition of women's human rights within the UN system, see chapter 3.

12. Annual Report, Inter-American Commission for Human Rights. 35, OAS/Ser.L./V./III. 19, doc. 13 (1988).

13. Romany, 1994, p. 100. For a more thorough discussion, see chapter 3.

14. Susan James, "The Good-Enough Citizen: Female Citizenship and Independence," in *Beyond Justice and Equality: Citizenship; Feminist Politics; Female Subjectivity,* eds. Gisela Bock and Susan James (New York: Routledge, 1992), p. 48.

15. For purposes of clarity, it is important to note here that ratification of international human rights treaties neither substantially compromises the sovereignty of the state nor would it result in immediate changes in the conditions of women's lives.

16. Catharine MacKinnon, *Feminism Unmodified: Discourses on Life and Law* (Cambridge, MA: Harvard University Press, 1987).

17. Jane Mansbridge, *Why We Lost the ERA* (Chicago: University of Chicago Press, 1986).

18. Jane M. Pickering, "Law and the Status of Women in the United States," in *Law and the Status of Women: An International Symposium,* ed. The Columbia Human Rights Law Review (1977): 311–344.

19. Adriana Cavarero, "Equality and Sexual Difference: Amnesia in Political Thought," in *Beyond Equality and Difference: Citizenship, Feminist Politics, Female Subjectivity,* eds. Gisela Bock and Susan James (New York: Routledge, 1992), p. 45.

20. Dorothy McBride Stetson, *Women's Rights in the U.S.A.: Policy Debates and Gender roles* (Pacific Grove, CA: Brooks/Cole, 1991), p. 31.

21. See chapter 5.

22. C. B. MacPherson, *The Life and Times of Liberal Democracy* (London: Oxford University Press, 1977), 19–20.

23. Ava Baron, "Feminist Legal Strategies: The Powers of Difference," in *Analyzing Gender: A Handbook of Social Science Research,* ed. Beth B. Hess and Myra Marx Ferree (Newbury Park, CA: Sage, 1987), pp. 474–503.

24. David P. Forsythe, *The Internationalization of Human Rights* (Lexington, KY: Lexington Books, 1991, p. 135.

25. Belinda Clark, "The Vienna Convention Reservations Regime and the Convention on Discrimination Against Women," *The American Journal of International Law,* vol. 85 (1991): 282–283. In this article, Clark reports that as of December 31, 1980, one hundred states were party to the Convention, of which forty-one had entered substantive reservations.

26. Laura Reanda, "UN Approach to Women's Rights," *Human Rights Quarterly,* John Hopkins University Press, vol. 3, no.1 (1981): 11–31.

27. John Gray, *Liberalism* (Minneapolis: University of Minnesota Press, 1986), pp. ix-xi.

28. Natalie K. Hevener, *International Law and the Status of Women* (Boulder, CO: Westview Press, 1983).

29. Charlesworth, 1994, pp. 58–84.

30. A/RES/2263 (XXII), November 7, 1967.

31. See also, Rebecca J. Cook, "Reservations to the Convention on the Elimination of all Forms of Discrimination against Women," *Virginia Journal of International Law,* vol. 30 (1990): 643–716.

32. Romany, 1994, pp. 85–115.

33. Leslie Calman, "Are Women's Rights 'Human Rights'?" Working paper 146 (New York: Barnard College, 1987).

34. Stetson, 1991, pp. 231–253.

35. Ibid.
36. Jyl Josephson, *Gender Families and the State: Child Support Policy in the United States* (Lanham, MD: Rowman and Littlefield, 1997).
37. In a case of gender discrimination, using the "suspect classification," the court would only allow a law to stand if the state could show a *compelling* state interest. Such a test is used in scrutinizing racially based laws, but has not been used to scrutinize gender-based restrictions.
38. Stetson, 1991, p. 37.
39. Romany, 1994, pp. 85–115.
40. See appendix.
41. Romany, 1994, pp. 85–115.
42. International legal precedence for this definition of complicity was established in *Rodriguez Velasquez* v. *Honduras* (1989) under a decision of the Inter-American Court of Human Rights.
43. CEDAW, UN Publication 84–44582.

Chapter 3

1. Committee on the Elimination of All Forms of Discrimination against Women, Meeting Statement, Vienna (1989).
2. Sarah Brown, "Feminism, International Theory, and International Relations of Gender Inequality," in *Millenium: Journal of International Studies*, vol. 17, no. 3 (1988): 461–75.
3. Ibid.
4. Ibid.
5. Felicia Gaer, "In Brief," *International Human Rights Abuses against Women: Hearing before the Subcommittee on Human Rights and International Organizations, House of Representatives,* 101st Cong., 2nd Sess., Mar 21 and July 26, 1990, p. 70: "while the international human rights community continues to struggles with the appropriateness of intrusion into private life—seen as possible rights violations—the CEDAW convention seeks precisely such intrusiveness. Moreover, while international human rights law and implementation mechanisms are ill-suited to deal with issues of covert structural violence, the CEDAW wants—indeed needs—to address such matters to extirpate many forms of gender-discrimination."
6. Rebecca Cook, in "Reservations to the Women's Convention," a paper delivered at the *International Women's Rights Action Watch (IWRAW) Loes Brunott Memorial Seminar,* New York, January 20, 1992, reported: "The UN office of Legal Affairs has advised, however, that CEDAW itself does not have the authority to decide whether the reservations are compatible with the object and purpose of the Women's Convention, nor directly to request the ICJ [International Court of Justice] to give an Advisory Opinion." ECOSOC has the authority to act on both counts, but for the reasons previously stated does not.

7. Belinda Clark, "The Vienna Convention Reservations Regime and the Convention on Discrimination against Women," in *The American Journal of International Law,* vol. 85 (1991): 282. "As of December 31, 1989, one hundred states were parties, of which forty-one had entered substantive reservations."

8. Clark, 1996.

9. Clark, 1991, p. 286.

10. Report of the Committee on the Elimination of Discrimination against Women on its Fifth Session, 41 UN GAOR Supp. (No. 45) at 46, UN Doc. A/41/45 (1986).

11. Rebecca Cook, "Reservations to the Women's Convention," a paper presented to the *International Women's Rights Action Watch (IWRAW) Loes Brunott Seminar,* 20 January 1992, New York City.

12. According to Rebecca Cook, in "Reservations to the Women's Convention": "The Women's Convention has the highest number of reservations of all the international human rights conventions."

13. The differences in women's experience across cultures and the tension created by their differing priorities in early efforts to universalize concern for women's rights is covered more fully in a later section of this chapter.

14. Elise Anette Grannes, "CEDAW # 9: A Report on the Ninth Session of the Committee on the Elimination of Discrimination against Women," *Journal of International Women's Rights Action Watch* (May 1990).

15. Clark, 1991, p. 286. "Since the reservations with the broadest scope had been entered by Bangladesh and Egypt and concerned conflict with the *Shari'a* (Islamic law), some delegations objected that the draft was anti-semitic."

16. Riane Eisler, "Human Rights: Toward an Integrated Theory for Action," *Human Rights Quarterly* vol. 9, no. 3 (1987): 287–308.

17. Ibid.

18. "From the Dais: Women's Rights Are Human Rights," *Human Rights Tribune* vol. 1, no. 4 (Winter 1993): 3: "In the UN, women's rights have always been bureaucratically isolated from human rights, reflecting what some view as a male-dominated bias regarding what constitutes a serious human rights abuse."

19. Experts believed that sovereignty would be the issue raised most frequently at the World Conference on Human Rights in June 1993 for the purpose of mitigating the effect of human rights instruments. See lecture by Philip Alston, representative from the United Nations Committee on Economic and Social Rights, at a press conference, National Press Club, Washington, DC (May 7, 1993). See also, "Where is the World Conference Going?" *Human Rights Tribune* vol. 1, no. 4 (Winter 1993): 5.

20. Gaer, 1990.

21. Hilkka Pietila and Jeanne Vickers, *Making Women Matter: The Role of the United Nations* (London: Zed Books, 1990).

22. Angela Miles, *Integrative Feminisms: Building Global Visions 1960's–1990's* (New York: Routledge, 1996), pp. 93–97.

23. Hilary Charlesworth, Christine Chinkin, and Shelley Wright, "Feminist Approaches to International Law," in *American Journal of International Law*, vol. 85 (1991): 621.

24. Clark, 1991, p. 284. See also, Margaret Galey, "International Enforcement of Women's Rights," *Human Rights Quarterly*, vol. 6 no. 4 (1984): 463–90.

25. Kathy E. Ferguson, "Women, Feminism and Development," in *Women, International Development and Politics*, ed. Kathleen Staudt (Philadelphia: Temple University Press, 1990), pp. 291–303.

26. Brown, 1988, p. 473.

27. Jack Donnelly, *International Human Rights* (Boulder, CO: Westview, 1993).

28. Natalie Hevener, in her *International Law and the Status of Women* (Boulder, Colorado: Westview, 1983), uses three analytical categories to describe and assess laws pertaining to women. These categories (protective, corrective, and sex-neutral) are offered as a perspective on the attitudes toward the rights of women in their respective countries.

29. Articles 16 and 25 of The Universal Declaration of Human Rights deal with the family and children. In Article 16, the family is identified as "the natural and fundamental group unit of society and is entitled to protection by society and the state." In Article 25, the words "himself and his family" endow a position of representation within the larger community, and also one of ownership upon "him." Use of the term "human beings" in the preamble, notwithstanding, the patriarchal structure of the family is reified in these articles—within which structure the position of woman is subordinate.

30. Kathleen Staudt, "Gender Politics in Bureaucracy: Theoretical Issues in Comparative Perspective," in *Women, International Development, and Politics*, ed. Kathleen Staudt (Philadelphia: Temple University Press, 1990).

31. David Matas, "The Canadian Council for Refugees—Twelve Recommendations on Gender Persecution," *Human Rights Tribune* vol. 1, no. 4 (Winter 1993): 32. (In the United States, there are several states that do not recognize spousal rape as a crime).

32. Hevener, 1983. See chapter 2 for further discussion of Hevener's categories: protective, corrective, nondiscriminatory.

33. "Violence against Women," *Women 2000*, no. 4 (1992).

34. See appendix.

35. Margaret Galey, "International Enforcement of Women's Rights," *Human Rights Quarterly*, vol. 6, no. 4 (1984): 463–90.

36. John Ward Anderson and Molly Moore, "Third World, Second Class: The Burden of Womenhood," *The Washington Post*, February 14, 1993, p. 1. This article is the first in a five-article series that describes the lives of women in South American, Indian, and Asian countries.

37. Leslie Calman in "Are Women's Rights 'Human Rights'?" (Barnard College: working paper # 146, 1987), p. 10, notes: "The 1979 Convention [CEDAW] is a significant improvement over the 1967 Declaration [DEDAW] in that it omits any language that proclaims the primacy of the family over the rights of the individuals who make up the family." And later, "The language giving priority to the family, however, has a much longer tradition in international law,

and whether the feminism of the 1979 document will be extended in the future remains to be seen." But as Calman says very clearly, " This is not to say that the family *per se* is the cause of all this; the family, in the socialist feminist critique, is an agent of control for much larger social forces, specifically capital and the state. Nonetheless, to strengthen the power of the family unit does not seem a strategy likely to benefit women; instead it would benefit those men who control women's labor and its products."

38. Johannes Morsink, "Women's Rights and the Universal Declaration," *Human Rights Quarterly*, vol. 13, no. 2 (1991): 229–256.

39. U.N. Document E/38/Rev.1/App.1 at 14.

40. C. B. Macpherson, *Life and Times of Liberal Democracy* (New York: Oxford University Press, 1977), p. 21.

41. Julia Preston, "Third World, Second Class: Women in the Village," *The Washington Post*, February 15, 1993, p. 1.

42. Charlesworth, 1991, p. 621.

43. Pietila and Vickers, 1990, p. 73: "Thus, IWY is one example of an NGO initiative taken up by the UN System—one which on this occasion exceeded all expectations, developing into a process with dimensions and repercussions such as the initiators had hardly dared to dream of [*sic*]."

44. Ibid., p. 122.

45. Ibid., p. 79.

46. Chilla Bulbeck. *One World Women's Movement* (London: Pluto Press, 1988), pp. 119–125.

47. Betty Friedan. *The Feminine Mystique* (New York: Dell, 1977).

48. See, Rosalinda Mendez Gonzalez, "Distinctions in Western Women's Experience: Ethnicity, Class, and Social Change," in *The Women's West*, eds. Susan Armitage and Elizabeth Jameson (Oklahoma City: University of Oklahoma Press, 1987). Also Audre Lorde, *Sister Outsider* (Freedom, CA: Crossing Press, 1984).

49. Angela Miles, *Integrative Feminisms* (New York: Routledge, 1996), pp. 109–117.

50. Marie Cardinal, *The Words to Say It* (Cambridge: VanVactor and Goodheart, 1983).

51. Elise Young, in *Keepers of the History: Women and the Israeli-Palestinian Conflict* (New York and London: Teacher's College Press, 1992), p. 6, says: "Women struggle for the right to equal access to male constructs: to economic systems, justice, education. They struggle within a social system and social reality defined and controlled for the benefit of those men with the most access to male power."

52. UN document A/Conf.11/28 dated September 15, 1985, para. 174,107,110,111, 117, 267, 120, 59.

53. "Forward Looking Strategies: For the Advancement of Women to the Year 2000," prepared from the English language edition of the *Report of the World Conference to Review and Appraise the Achievements of the United Nations Decade for Women: Equality, Development,and Peace*, issued as UN document A/Conf.11/28 dated September 15, 1985.

54. Clark, 1991, p. 285.

55. The sense in which the term hegemonic is used is that in which one state or region dominates the discourse.

56. Catharine MacKinnon, *Feminism Unmodified: Discourses on Life and Law* (Cambridge, MA: Harvard University Press, 1989), pp. 38–39.

57. Audre Lorde made these comments at a meeting of the Second Sex Conference in New York University Institute for the Humanities, September 29, 1979. They are also included in the chapter "The Master's Tools Will Never Dismantle the Master's House," *Sister Outsider: Essays and Speeches by Audre Lorde* (New York: The Crossing Press, 1984).

58. Lorde, 1984.

59. See Jane Flax's argument in *Beyond Equality and Difference: Citizenship; Feminist Politics; Female Subjectivity*, eds. Gisela Bock and Susan James (New York: Routledge, 1992), pp. 193–210.

60. Chilla Bulbeck, "Equality, Politics and Gender," *One World Women's Movement* (London: Pluto, 1988).

61. *The Forward Looking Strategies to the Year 2000* came out of the 1985 World Conference for Women in Nairobi.

62. *The World Plan of Action* was the set of agreements developed in Copenhagen in 1980 at the Mid-Decade World Conference for Women.

63. Rebecca Cook, in an unpublished paper entitled, "Reservations to the Women's Convention," presented to the *International Women's Rights Action Watch (IWRAW) Loes Brunott Memorial Seminar,* January 20, 1992, noted that " . . . more than 80 substantive reservations have been made to the Convention on the Elimination of All Forms of Discrimination Against Women (the Women's Convention). These reservations dilute the international norm of the prohibition of all forms of discrimination against women. They devalue the international currency with respect to women's rights. In other words, the Women's Convention looks like a piece of Swiss cheese with lots of wholes [*sic*] and exceptions."

64. For a thorough review of the Vienna Convention on Law of Treaties, the changes it has made in the reservations regime and the effect those changes have had on human rights treaties in general (and CEDAW specifically) see Clark, 1991, pp. 289–321.

65. Galey, 1984, pp. 463–489.

66. UN document A/Conf. 11/28.

67. Nancy Hartsock, "Feminist Theory and the Development of Revolutionary Strategy," in *Capitalist Patriarchy and the Case for Socialist Feminism,* ed. Z. R. Eisenstein (New York: Monthly Review Press, 1979), pp. 56, 58.

68. See appendix.

69. Congress, House of Representatives, *International Human Rights Abuses against Women: Hearing before the Subcommittee on Human Rights and International Organizations* ("In Brief," by Felicia Gaer), 101st Cong., 2nd Sess., March 21 and July 26, 1990.

70. Ibid.

71. Clark, 1991, p. 286.

72. Barbara Lewis, "Farming Women, Public Policy, and the Women's Ministry: A Case Study from Cameroon," in *Women, International Development, and Politics,* ed. Kathleen Staudt (Philadelphia: Temple University Press, 1990), pp. 180–200. Not until the World Conference on Women in Beijing, China, in 1995, were the productive and reproductive efforts of women included in the overall gross national product of their specific countries.

73. Zillah Eisenstein, *The Color of Gender: Reimaging Democracy* (Berkeley: University of California Press, 1994). Eisenstein argues, for instance, that every woman has a universal human right to control her body, yet this right must be specified in terms of a woman's differing circumstances, such as her ability to get pregnant.

74. Jack Donnelly, in "Cultural Relativism and Universal Human Rights," *Human Rights Quarterly* vol. 6, no. 4 (1984): 403, recognizes that universalism and cultural relativism lie along a continuum, but, he says, "A cultural relativist account of human rights, however, seems to be guilty of logical contradiction. If human rights are based in human nature, on the simple fact that one is a human being, and if human nature is universal, then how can human rights be relative in any fundamental way?"

75. *Women, International Development, and Politics,* ed. Kathleen Staudt (Philadelphia: Temple University Press, 1990).

76. Karin Himmelstrand, in "Can an Aid Bureaucracy Empower Women?" in *Women, International Development, and Politics,* ed. Staudt, p. 112, is very clear: "When it comes to the empowerment of women, grassroots associations play an absolutely crucial role. It will take time before they reach that goal, but an important process has been started. Many times the process itself is more important for empowerment than reaching the specific goal. By solving problems, gaining experience, and working together, women will become aware of their own subordinate position in society and more capable of changing it."

77. Eisenstein, 1994.

78. Ibid., p. 17

79. Staudt, 1990.

80. Hibaaq Osman, Tammy Horn, and Diana Zoelle (unpublished) "The Project for Women to Bring Peace, Democracy, and Human Rights to Somalia," (Washington, DC: Women's Program, Fund for Peace, 1995).

Chapter 4

1. Virginia Woolf, *Three Guineas* (San Diego: Harcourt, Brace, 1938).

2. Gary Gereffi, "Power and Dependency in an Interdependent World," in *Global Crisis: Sociological Analyses and Responses,* ed. Edward. A. Tiryakian (The Netherlands: E.J. Brill, 1984).

3. This assertion is in no way a denial or underestimation of other states' influence in the global community. Neither is it an attempt to establish U.S.

power as an immutable force in international relations. The United States and its behavior in relation to the promotion of human rights is the focus of this study, an effort to think about ways to improve an improvable system. Any reference to or comparison with other states is purely for contextual purposes.

4. Jack Donnelly, *International Human Rights, Dilemmas in World Politics* (Boulder, CO: Westview, 1993), p. 7.

5. Nigel Rodley, "On the Necessity of United States Ratification of International Human Rights Conventions," in *U.S. Ratification of Human Rights Treaties: With or Without Reservations?*, ed. Richard B. Lillich (Charlottesville: University Press of Virginia, 1981), pp. 3–19.

6. Diane F. Orentlicher, "The United States Commitment to International Human Rights," *Human Rights and the World Community: Issues and Action*, 2nd ed., eds. Richard Pierre Claude and Burns H. Weston (Philadelphia: University of Pennsylvania Press, 1992), pp. 340–357.

7. David P. Forsythe, *Human Rights and World Politics* (Lincoln: University of Nebraska Press, 1983), p. 89.

8. Jeane J. Kirkpatrick, *Dictatorships and Double Standards: Pationalism and Reason in Politics* (New York: Simon and Shuster, 1982), p.8.

9. C. B. MacPherson, *The Real World of Democracy* (Oxford, UK: Clarendon Press, 1966).

10. David P. Forsythe, "Congress and Human Rights in U.S. Foreign Policy," *Human Rights Quarterly*, vol. 9, no. 3 (August 1987): 403.

11. George Soros, *The Crisis of Global Capitalism: Open Society Endangered* (New York: Perseus, 1998), p. xxii.

12. Orentlicher, 1992, p. 352.

13. Michael Clough, *Global Changes and Institutional Transformation: Restructuring the Foreign Policymaking Process*, Report of the 33rd Strategy for Peace, U.S. Foreign Policy Conference (Muscatine IA: The Stanley Foundation, 1992), pp. 8–9.

14. Soros, 1998, p. 102.

15. Ibid., xxx.

16. Hilary Charlesworth, "What Are 'Women's International Human Rights'?" in *Human Rights of Women: National and International Perspectives*, ed. Rebecca J. Cook (Philadelphia: University of Pennsylvania Press, 1994).

17. C. B. MacPherson, in *The Real World of Democracy* (Oxford, UK: Clarendon Press, 1966), pp. 56–67, makes the argument that underdeveloped countries have undertaken the conquest of material scarcity by methods other than the acquisitive, individual power-seeking methods of the market societies. "They are trying to overcome scarcity without relying on the morality of scarcity."

18. Ibid., p. 67.

19. Clough, 1992, p.7.

20. Ibid., 8–9.

21. The President of the United States, *Four Treaties Pertaining to Human Rights: the International Convention on the Elimination of All Forms of Racial Discrimination, the International Covenant on Economic Social and Cultural*

Rights, the International Covenant on Civil and Political Rights, and the American Convention on Human Rights, 95th Cong., 2nd Sess., Feb 23, 1978 (Washington, DC: Government Printing Office).

22. The President of the United States, *Convention on the Elimination of All Forms of Discrimination against Women,* 96th Cong., 2nd Sess., Nov 12, 1980 (Washington, DC: Government Printing Office).

23. Linda Tarr-Whelan, director of the Center for Policy Alternatives, Washington, D.C., now serves in a restricted capacity as liaison to the Commission.

24. In an address to the UN Security Council at the United Nations on January 20, 2000, Senator Jesse Helms is quoted by the Washington Post. He is articulating what sounds alarmingly like the rhetoric of the Bricker Amendment in the 1950's. For a thorough discussion of the Bricker Amendment, see Natalie Hevener Kaufman and David Whiteman, "Opposition to Human Rights Treaties in the United States Senate: The Legacy of the Bricker Amendment," *Human Rights Quarterly,* vol. 10, no. 3 (1988): 309–337.

25. William Schneider, CNN, "Play of the Week," June 12, 1999.

26. Rebecca J. Cook, "State Accountability Under the Convention on the Elimination of All Forms of Discrimination against Women," in *Human Rights of Women: National and International Perspectives,* ed. Rebecca J. Cook (Philadelphia: University of Pennsylvania Press, 1994), pp. 229–256.

27. Ambassador Madeleine Albright, U.S. permanent representative to the United Nations; chair, U.S. Delegation to the Fourth World Conference on Women, "The Fourth World Conference: A Success for the World's Women," in *Bringing Beijing Home* (Washington DC: Government Printing Office, January 1996).

28. Soros, 1998, p. 84.

29. Richard Falk, "Theoretical Foundations of Human Rights," in *Human Rights and the World Community,* eds. Richard P. Claude and Burns H. Weston (Philadelphia: University of Pennsylvania Press, 1992).

30. Hilary Charlesworth, 1994, pp. 58–84.

31. Celina Romany, "State Responsibility Goes Private: A Feminist Critique of the Public/Private Distinction in International Human Rights Law," in *Human Rights of Women: National and International Perspectives,* ed. Rebecca J. Cook (Philadelphia: University of Pennsylvania Press, 1994), p. 85.

32. 28 I.L.M. 294 (1989). According to Romany, 1994, pp. 101–102.

33. The case of *Velasquez Rodriguez* v. *Honduras* and the meaning of the case for protection of women is discussed in more depth in chapter 2.

34. Zillah Eisenstein, *The Color of Gender: Reimaging Democracy* (Berkeley: University of California Press, 1994), pp. 15–35.

35. D. Forsythe, 1983, p. 138.

36. Falk, 1992.

37. Professor Edy Kaufman, University of Maryland Department of Government and Politics Lecture (GOVT 808B): February 4, 1993.

38. Forsythe, 1983, pp. 383–389.

39. Ibid., 385.

150 Globalizing Concern for Women's Human Rights

40. Laurie S. Wiseberg and Harry M. Scoble, "Monitoring Human Rights Violations: The Role of Nongovernmental Organizations," in *Human Rights and Foreign Policy*, eds. Donald Kommers and Gilbert Loescher (Notre Dame, IN: University of Notre Dame Press, 1979).

41. See, Richard L. Rubenstein, *The Cunning of History* (New York: Harper Colophon, 1975), p.6: "The Holocaust was an expression of some of the most significant political, moral, religious and demographic tendencies of Western civilization in the twentieth century."

42. These definitions are more complex than is indicated here, but essentially require that the person's act was "political" in nature, the person had not used nor advocated violence in his/her "crime" and that his/her effort had been one of "last resort."

43. Wiseberg and Scoble, 1979, pp. 185–186.

44. Clyde Collins Snow, Eric Stover, and Kari Hannibal, "Scientists as Detectives: Investigating Human Rights," in *Human Rights and the World Community*, eds. Richard P. Claude and Burns H. Weston (Philadelphia: University of Pennsylvania Press), pp. 384–391.

45. Felicia Gaer, "Reality Check: Human Rights NGOs Confront Governments at the UN," in *NGOs, the UN, and Global Governance*, eds. Thomas G. Weiss and Leon Gordenker (Boulder, CO: Lynne Rienner, 1996), pp. 51–66.

46. MacPherson, 1966, p.50.

47. Ibid., 67.

48. The World Conference on Human Rights was held in June 1993, in Vienna, Austria.

49. MacPherson, supra note 43 at 62.

50. See, for example, Jeane Kirkpatrick, *Dictatorships and Double Standards: Rationalism and Reason in Politics* (New York: Simon and Schuster, 1982).

51. Clough, 1992.

52. Natalie Hevener Kaufman and David Whiteman, "Opposition to Human Rights Treaties in the United States Senate: The Legacy of the Bricker Amendment," *Human Rights Quarterly*, vol. 10, no. 3 (1988): 309–337.

53. D. Forsythe, 1983, pp. 119–142.

54. David P. Forsythe, "Congress and Human Rights in U.S. Foreign Policy: The Fate of General Legislation," *Human Rights Quarterly*, vol. 9, no. 3 (1987): pp. 382–404.

55. Vamik Volkan, *The Need For Enemies and Allies* (Dunmore, PA: Jason Aronson, 1994).

56. Richard P. Claude, "The Case of Joelito Filartiga in the Courts," in *Human Rights and the World Community*, eds. Richard P. Claude and Burns H. Weston (Philadelphia: University of Pennsylvania Press, 1992), pp. 328–337.

57. Ibid.

58. Claude, 1992, p. 333.

59. Jack Donnelly, *Universal Human Rights in Theory and Practice*, ch. 6 (Ithaca, NY: Cornell University Press, 1989).

Chapter 5

1. Jane Flax, "Beyond Equality: Gender, Justice and Difference," in *Beyond Equality and Difference: Citizenship; Feminist Politics; Female Subjectivity,* eds. Gisela Bock and Susan James (New York: Routledge, 1992), pp. 193–210.

2. Dorothy McBride Stetson, *Women's Rights in the U.S.A.: Policy Debates and Gender Roles* (Pacific Grove, CA: Brooks/Cole, 1991). See also, Ilka Tanya Payan, "Women's Human Rights in the United States: An Immigrant's Perspective," in *Women's Rights Human Rights: International Feminist Perspectives,* eds. Julie Peters and Andrea Wolper (New York: Routledge, 1995), pp. 82–88.

3. David Forsythe, *Internationalization of Human Rights* (Lexington, KY: Lexington Books, 1991), p. 121. In his chapter entitled "Human Rights and the United States: Exceptionalism and International Society" (pp. 119–142), Forsythe speaks to the issue of the United States and its history of exceptionalism. I argue here that the U.S. notion of human rights limits itself, virtually exclusively, to civil and political rights.

4. The International Covenant on Economic, Social, and Cultural Rights (1976) was presented by President Clinton for advice and consent in 1994. Since the convening of the 104th Congress, no action has been taken, no hearings have been held, and no mention has been made.

5. Evidence of U.S. ambivalence toward civil rights can be found in the current move by states to dismantle affirmative action programs. The programs that were set in place to achieve equality may be faulty; the attempt to achieve parity is not. Little concerted effort has been made to discover alternatives to affirmative action as it was instituted in the 1960s. Proponents of anti-affirmative action legislation proclaim that parity has been achieved and that continued efforts to promote proportional representation of women and minorities in higher education and in the workplace is itself discriminatory.

6. See chapter 4.

7. Marguerite Guzman Bouvard, *Women Reshaping Human Rights: How Extraordinary Activists Are Changing the World* (Wilmington, DE: Scholarly Resources, 1996), p. 237.

8. Catharine MacKinnon, *Feminism Unmodified: Discourses on Life and Law* (Cambridge, MA: Harvard University Press, 1987).

9. *Women in the Politics of Postcommunist Eastern Europe,* ed. Marilyn Rueschemeyer (New York: M.E. Sharpe, 1994). See also, *Women Transforming Politics: Worldwide Strategies for Empowerment,* ed. Jill M. Bystydzienski (Bloomington: Indiana University Press, 1992).

10. Shelley Wright, "Economic Rights, Social Justice and the State: A Feminist Reappraisal," in *Reconceiving Reality: Women and International Law,* ed. Dorinda G. Dallmeyer (Washington, DC: The American Society of International Law, 1993."

11. Zillah Eisenstein, *The Color of Gender: Reimaging Democracy* (Berkeley: University of California Press, 1994), p. 16.

12. I argue in chapter 1 that unreserved ratification of the International Convention on the Elimination of All Forms of Discrimination against Women (1981) and adherence to its intent would afford a "common language" for states party to begin to address this universal problem within their un-common cultural settings. The failure of mainstream human rights documents to address the harms of women is set forth very clearly by Hilary Charlesworth: "What Are 'Women's International Human Rights'?" in *Human Rights of Women: National and International Perspectives* (Philadelphia: University of Pennsylvania Press, 1994), pp. 58–84.

13. Eisenstein, 1994, p. 18.

14. Francis Fukuyama, *The End of History and the Last Man* (New York: Free Press, 1992).

15. C. B. MacPherson, *The Life and Times of Liberal Democracy* (New York: Oxford University Press, 1977), p.7.

16. Eisenstein, 1994, p. 173.

17. Jack Donnelly, *Universal Human Rights in Theory and Practice* (Ithaca, NY: Cornell University Press, 1989).

18. David Campbell, "Foreign Policy and Identity: Japanese 'Other'/American Self," in *The Global Economy as Political Space*, eds. Stephen J. Rosow, Naeem Inayatullah and Mark Rupert (Boulder, CO: Lynne Rienner, 1994), pp. 147–169.

19. Robin West, *Narrative, Authority, and Law* (Ann Arbor: The University of Michigan Press, 1993), p. 47.

20. Flax, 1992, pp. 192–210.

21. West, 1993, pp. 184–189.

22. John Gray, *Liberalism* (Minneapolis: University of Minnesota Press, 1995). The distinctions are also made very clearly by Norberto Bobbio in *Liberalism and Democracy* (New York: Verso, 1990), and by Isaiah Berlin in *Four Essays on Liberalism* (New York: Oxford University Press, 1969).

23. Gray, 1995, p. x.

24. In compositing this word I wish to convey, not simply gender distinctions, but the various nature of human beings. Another form of exclusivity is created when efforts to include women in the public space do not incorporate these various immutable dimensions of being.

25. Flax, 1992, p. 197.

26. Ibid. In this context, my understanding of the ideals of culture relies heavily on Jane Flax's argument. Culture develops, according to Flax, in that "space" created through interaction of self and other—or self and world. In chapter 1, and more explicitly in chapter 2, I make the argument that the U.S. system has developed in the absence of real concern for the rights of women. As a consequence of women having privately asserted their rights there has developed an ever-widening disjuncture between women's lived experience and women's systemically ascribed roles.

27. Barbara R. Bergmann, *In Defense of Affirmative Action* (New York: Harper-Collins, 1996).

28. This argument is illustrated by, Jean Bethke Elshtain, *Democracy on Trial* (New York: HarperCollins, 1995). Also see, David Blankenhorn, *Fatherless America* (New York: Basic Books, 1995).

29. Chapter 3 discusses the ways that women—even strong advocates of women's human rights—failed to recognize the stultifying effects of employing the neutral "he" in drafting human rights legislation.

30. Mary Ann Glendon, *Rights Talk: the Impoverishment of Political Discourse* (New York: The Free Press, 1991). See also, Audre Lorde, *Sister Outsider: Essays and Speeches* (Freedom, CA: Crossing Press, 1984).

31. Chapter 3 provides a more thorough analysis of women's struggle to recognize their differences and their commonalities.

32. Seyla Benhabib, in *Situating the Self: Gender, Community and Postmodernism in Contemporary Ethics* (New York: Routledge, 1992), pp. 214–218, says: "Surely we can criticize the 'metaphysical suppositions of identity politics' and challenge the supremacy of heterosexist positions in the women's movement. Yet is such a challenge only thinkable via a complete debunking of any concepts of selfhood, agency and autonomy?" (Also, chapter 3 of this text discusses differing perspectives based on race and class.)

33. Eisenstein, 1994.

34. Andrea L. Bonnicksen, in *Civil Rights and Liberties* (Palo Alto, CA: Mayfield, 1982), p 143, cites *Levy* v. *Louisiana* (1968) as an illustration of the invisibility of private relationship: Upon her wrongful death, Levy's children could not recover damages, because they were illegitimate. Only legitimate children could file for damages in a wrongful death case. What is at issue in the decision is the absence of the state-proscribed, *public* relationship of the children to their mother. The state proscription preempts, and thus fails to reveal, the *private* reliance of the children on their mother.

35. Barbara Hobson, in "Childcare and Types of Welfare States," in *Gendering Welfare States* (London: Sage, 1994), pp. 45–61, discusses "solo mothers" in the United States. She claims that "seldom did black families receive benefits" and "there were usually restrictions on benefits to never married women."

36. Virginia Sapiro, "The Gender Basis of American Social Policy," in *Women, the State, and Welfare,* ed. Linda Gordon (Madison: University of Wisconsin Press, 1990), pp. 36–54.

37. Linda Gordon, "Family Violence, Feminism, and Social Control," in *Women, the State and Welfare,* ed. Linda Gordon (Madison: University of Wisconsin Press, 1990), pp. 178–198.

38. Nancy Fraser and Linda Nicholson, "Social Criticism Without Philosophy: An Encounter Between Feminism and Postmodernism," in *Feminism/Postmodernism,* ed. Linda J. Nicholson (New York: Routledge, 1990), p. 29. See also, Diane Sainsbury, "Women's and Men's Social Rights: Gendering Dimensions of Welfare States," in *Gendering Welfare States* (London: Sage, 1994), pp. 150–169.

39. Ibid., p. 35.

40. Catharine A. MacKinnon, "Not by Law Alone: From a Debate with Phyllis Schlafly," in *Feminism Unmodified: Discourses on Life and Law* (Cambridge, MA: Harvard University Press, 1987).

41. Robin West, "Women's Hedonic Lives," in *Narrative, Authority, and the Law* (Ann Arbor: University of Michigan Press, 1993), pp. 179–249.

42. C. B. MacPherson, *The Political Theory of Possessive Individualism: Hobbes to Locke* (New York: Oxford University Press, 1962), p. 144. "These economic rights, like the civil and religious rights, were demanded for everyone. In practice, of course, the rights to produce, trade &c.,[*sic*] could be enjoyed only by those who had the disposal of their own labor."

43. *Beyond Equality & Difference: Citizenship, Feminist Politics, and Female Subjectivity,* ed. Gisela Bock and Susan James (New York: Routledge, 1992). In her article, "Beyond Equality: Gender, Justice and Difference," Flax poses the problem of justice and its meaninglessness in an unjust context. In this case, "unlikes" competing for (just) acquisition in a system arranged to privilege "likes."

44. C. B. MacPherson, *The Life and Times of Liberal Democracy* (New York: Oxford University Press, 1977), p. 88.

45. Tanya Melich, "Creation of the Republican party," in *The Republican War Against Women* (New York: Bantam Books. 1996).

46. *Second Treatise of Government,* ed. Thomas P. Peardon (New York: Macmillan, 1952), pp. 96–99.

47. MacPherson, 1977.

48. Jean Bethke Elshtain, *The Color of Gender: Reimaging Democracy* (Berkeley: University of California Press, 1994), p. 40.

49. Joseph Raz offers a comprehensive explication of the forms and structural facilitations of autonomy in his text, *Morality of Freedom* (Oxford, UK: Clarendon Press, 1986).

50. Jane Mansbridge, *Why We Lost the ERA* (Chicago: Chicago University Press, 1986).

51. Frederick Thayer, *An End to Hierarchy! An End to Competition!: Organizing the Politics and Economics of Survival* (New York: New Viewpoints, 1973).

52. Fraser and Nicholson, 1990, pp. 19–38.

53. In this context "constitutionally" refers to the legal document, and is a response, albeit indirect, to the text of Robert A. Goldwin, *Why Blacks, Women and Jews Are Not Mentioned in the Constitution, and Other Unorthodox Views* (Lanham, MD: AEI Press, 1990).

54. Ibid.

55. Evelyn Fox Keller, *Reflections on Science and Gender* (New Haven, CT: Yale University Press, 1985). Keller argues that the "masculinization of science" has served (1) to exclude women from participation in scientific endeavor and (2) to circumscribe, very particularly, the focus of the endeavor itself.

56. Christine Sylvester, "Feminists and Realists View Autonomy and Obligation in International Relations," in *Gendered States: Feminist (Re)Visions of Inter-*

national Relations, ed. V. Spike Peterson (Boulder, CO: Lynne Rienner, 1992), pp. 155–178.

57. Keller, 1985, p. 99.

58. Susan James, "The Good-Enough Citizen," *Beyond Equality and Difference: Citizenship, Feminist Politics, Female Subjectivity,* eds. Gisela Bock and Susan James (New York: Routledge, 1992), pp. 48–65.

59. *Women's Rights in the United States: A Documentary History,* eds. Winston E. Langley and Vivian C. Fox (Westport, CT: Greenwood Press, 1994).

60. Jyl Josephson, *Gender, Families and the State: Child Support Policy in the United States* (Lanham, MD: Rowman and Littlefield Publishers, 1997).

61. Nancy Hartsock, "Foucault on Power," in *Feminism/Postmodernism,* ed. Linda J. Nicholson (New York: Routledge, 1990). In this article, Hartsock questions what a "theory of power" for women might look like. She is particularly sensitive to the reductive nature of previous theorizing about "women's" oppression. Robin West, in *Narrative, Authority, and Law* (Ann Arbor: University of Michigan Press, 1993), seems to argue for a situation-specific altruism in communal acts of power. Jyl Josephson investigates the U.S. system and is critical of the ways positive action by the state to alleviate women's oppression entails increased social and economic control over their (otherwise private) decisions.

62. Robin West, *Narrative, Authority and Law* (Ann Arbor: University of Michigan Press, 1993), pp. 175–76.

63. Natalie Hevener, *International law and the Status of Women* (Boulder, CO: Westview, 1983).

64. See chapter 1.

65. See appendix.

66. Jyl J. Josephson, *Gender Families and the State: Child Support Policy in the United States* (Lanham, MD: Rowman and Littlefield, 1997).

Bibliography

Albright, Ambassador Madeleine, "The Fourth World Conference: A Success for the World's Women," *Bringing Beijing Home* (Washington, DC: Government Printing Office, January 1996).

Arnaud, A. J., and E. Kingdom, eds., *Women's Rights and the Rights of Man* (Edinburgh: Aberdeen University Press, 1990).

Baron, Ava, "Feminist Legal Strategies: The Powers of Difference," in *Analyzing Gender: A Handbook of Social Science Research,* eds. Beth B. Hess and Myra Marx Ferree (Newbury Park, CA: Sage, 1987).

Bartlett, Donald L, and James B. Steele, *America: What Went Wrong?* (Kansas City, MO: Andrews and McMeel, 1992).

Basic Facts about the United Nations, Department of Public Information (New York: United Nations, 1995).

Benhabib, Seyla, *Situating the Self: Gender, Community and Postmodernism in Contemporary Ethics* (New York: Routledge, 1992).

Bergmann, Barbara R., *In Defense of Affirmative Action* (New York: HarperCollins, 1996).

Berlin, Isaiah, *Four Essays on Liberty* (New York: Oxford University Press, 1969).

Black, Naomi, and Ann Baker Cottrell, eds., *Women and World Change: Equity Issues in Development* (Beverly Hills, CA: Sage, 1981).

Blankenhorn, David, *Fatherless America* (New York: Basic Books, 1989).

Bobbio, Norberto, *Liberalism and Democracy* (London and New York: Verso, 1990).

———*The Future of Democracy* (Minnesota: University of Minnesota Press, 1987).

Bonnicksen, Andrea L, *Civil Rights and Liberties* (Palo Alto, CA: Mayfield, 1982).

Bouvard, Marguerite Guzman, *Women Reshaping Human Rights: How Extraordinary Activists are Changing the World* (Wilmington, DE: Scholarly Resources, 1996).

Brogan, D. W., *The American Character* (New York: Time Incorporated, 1962).

Brown, Sarah, "Feminism, International Theory, and International Relations of Gender Inequality," *Millenium: Journal of International Studies* vol. 17, no. 3 (1988).

Bulbeck, Chilla, *One World Women's Movement,* London: Pluto Press, 1988.

Bunch, Charlotte, "Women's Rights as Human Rights: Toward a Revision of Human Rights," *Human Rights Quarterly,* vol. 12 no. 4 (1990): 486–498.

Bystydzienski, Jill M., ed., *Women Transforming Politics: Worldwide Strategies for Empowerment* (Bloomington: Indiana University Press, 1992).

Calman, Leslie J., *"Are Women's Rights 'Human Rights?'"* (Barnard College: Working Paper # 146, September 1987).

Campbell, David, "Foreign Policy and Identity: The Japanese 'Other'/American 'Self'," in *The Global Economy as Political Space,* eds. Stephen J. Rosow, Naeem Inayatullah, and Mark Rupert (Boulder, CO: Lynne Rienner, 1994), pp. 147–169.

Cassese, Antonio, *International Law in a Divided World* (Oxford: Clarendon Press, 1986).

Charlesworth, Hilary, "What Are 'Women's International Human Rights'?" in *Human Rights of Women: National and International Perspectives,* ed. Rebecca J. Cook (Philadelphia: University of Pennsylvania Press, 1994).

———, Christine Chinkin, and Shelley Wright. "Feminist Approaches to International Law," *American Journal of International Law,* vol. 85 (1991).

Chow, Esther Ngan-ling, and Catherine White Berheide, eds., *Women, the Family, and Policy: A Global Perspective* (Albany, NY: State University of New York Press, 1994).

Christman, John, ed., *The Inner Citadel: Essays on Individual Autonomy* (New York: Oxford University Press, 1989).

Clark, Janet M., ed., *Women and Politics* (New York: Haworth Press, 1995).

Claude, Richard P., "The Case of Joelito Filartiga in the Courts," *Human Rights and the World Community: Issues and Action,* 2nd. ed. eds., Richard Pierre Claude and Burns H. Weston (Philadelphia: University of Pennsylavania Press, 1992).

Cone, James H., *Martin and Malcolm and America: A Dream or a Nightmare?* (Maryknoll, NY: Orbis, 1993).

Congress, United States House of Representatives, Committee on Foreign Affairs, *International Human Rights Abuses Against Women: Hearing before the Subcommittee on Human Rights and International Organizations,* 101st Cong., 2nd Sess., March 21 and July 26, 1991 (Washington, DC: Government Printing Office, 1991).

Congress, United States House of Representatives Subcommittee on Human Rights and International Organizations, *International Human Rights abuses Against Women,* 101st Congr., 2nd Sess., March 21, and July 26, 1990 (Washington, DC: Government Printing Office, 1991).

Congress, United States Senate Committee on Foreign Relations, *Convention on the Elimination of All Forms of Discrimination against Women,* 101st Congr., 2nd Sess., August 2, 1990 (Washington, DC: Government Printing Office, 1991).

Cook, Rebecca J., "State Accountability Under the Convention on the Elimination of All Forms of Discrimination Against Women," *Human Rights of Women: National and International Perspectives,* ed. Rebecca J. Cook (Philadelphia: University of Pennsylvania Press, 1994).

———, ed., *Human Rights of Women: National and International Perspectives* (Philadelphia: University of Pennsylvania Press, 1994).

———"The International Right to Nondiscrimination on the Basis of Sex: A Bibliography," *Yale Journal of International Law,* vol. 14, no. 1 (1989): 161–181.

Donnelly, Jack, "Humanitarian Intervention and American Foreign Policy: Law, Morality and Politics," *Human Rights in the World Community: Issues and Action,* eds. Richard Pierre Claude and Burns H. Weston (Philadelphia: University of Pennsylvania Press, 1992).

———*Universal Human Rights in Theory and Practice* (Ithaca, NY: Cornell University Press, 1989).

———*International Human Rights* (Philadelphia: University of Pennsylvania Press, 1993).

———*International Human Rights: Dilemmas in World Politics* (Boulder, CO: Westview, 1993).

Doyal, Len, and Ian Gough, *A Theory of Human Need* (New York: Guilford, 1991).

Eisenstein, Zillah, *The Color of Gender: Reimaging Gender* (Los Angeles: University of California Press, 1994).

———*The Female Body and the Law* (Los Angeles: University of California Press, 1988).

Elshtain, Jean Bethke, *Public Man, Private Woman: Women in Social and Political Thought* (Princeton, NJ: Princeton University Press, 1981).

———*Democracy on Trial* (New York: HarperCollins, 1995).

———"Single Motherhood: A Response to Iris Marion Young," *Dissent* (Spring 1994).

Enloe, Cynthia. *Bananas, Beaches & Bases: Making Feminist Sense of International Politics* (Berkeley: University of California Press, 1989).

Falk, Richard, "Theoretical Foundations of Human Rights," in *Human Rights and the World Community,* eds. Richard P. Claude and Burns H. Weston (Philadelphia: University of Pennsylvania Press, 1992).

Forsythe, David P, *The Internationalization of Human Rights* (Lexington, KY: Lexington, 1991).

———*Human Rights and World Politics,* (Lincoln: University of Nebraska Press, 1983).

———"Congress and Human Rights in U.S. Foreign Policy: The Fate of General Legislation," *Human Rights Quarterly,* vol. 9, no. 3 (August 1987).

Fukuyama, Francis, *The End of History and the Last Man* (New York: Free Press, 1992).

Funk, Nanette, and Magda Mueller, eds., *Gender Politics and Post-Communism: Reflections from Eastern Europe and the Former Soviet Union* (New York: Routledge, 1993).

Galey, Margaret E., "International Enforcement of Women's Rights," *Human Rights Quarterly* vol. 6, no. 4 (1984): 463–90.

Gereffi, Gary, "Power and Dependency in an Interdependent World," *Global Crisis: Sociological Analyses and Responses,* ed. Edward A. Tiryakian (The Netherlands: E. J. Brill, 1984).

Gibney, Mark, ed., *World Justice?: U.S. Courts and International Human Rights* (Boulder, CO: Westview, 1991).

Glendon, Mary Ann. *Rights Talk: The Impoverishment of Political Discourse* (New York: Free Press, 1991).

Goldin, Claudia. *Understanding the Gender Gap: An Economic History of American Women* (New York: Oxford University Press, 1990).

Goldwin, Robert A. *Why Blacks, Women, and Jews Are Not Mentioned in the Constitution, and Other Unorthodox Views* (Washington, DC: AEI Press, 1990).

Gordon, Linda, *Heroes of Their Own Lives* (New York: Penguin, 1989).

———, "Family Violence, Feminism, and the Social Control," *Women, the State, and Welfare,* ed. Linda Gordon (Madison: University of Wisconsin Press, 1990).

———, ed., *Women, the State, and Welfare,* (Madison: University of Wisconsin Press, 1990).

Grannes, Elise Anette, "CEDAW # 9: A Report on the Ninth Session of the Committee on the Elimination of Discrimination against Women," *Journal of International Women's Rights Action Watch* (Minneapolis, MN: Humphrey Institute May 1990).

Gray, John, *Liberalism* (Minneapolis: University of Minnesota Press, 1995).

Halberstam, Malvina, and Elizabeth F. Defeis, *Women's Legal Rights: International Covenants—An Alternative to ERA?* (New York: Transnational, 1987).

Hanmer, Jalna, and Sheila Saunders, *Well-Founded Fear: A Community Study of Violence to Women* (London: Hutchinson, 1984).

Hannum, Hurst, "Self-Determination as a Human Right," in *Human Rights and the World Community: Issues and Action,* 2nd. ed., eds. Richard Pierre Claude and Burns H. Weston (Philadelphia: University of Pennsylvania Press, 1992).

Hartsock, Nancy, "Feminist Theory and the Development of Revolutionary Strategy," *Capitalist Patriarchy and the Case for Socialist Feminism,* ed. Z. R. Eisenstein (New York: Monthly Review Press, 1979).

Heilbrun, Carolyn G., *Reinventing Womanhood* (New York: W. W. Norton, 1979).

Hevener, Natalie, *International Law and the Status of Women,* (Boulder, CO: Westview Press, 1983).

Iglitzin, Lynne B., and Ruth Ross, eds., *Women in the World,* 2nd. ed. (Beverly Hills, CA: ABC-Clio, 1986).

The International Convention on the Elimination of All Forms of Discrimination against Women (New York: United Nations Publication 84-44582, 1990).

James, Susan, "The Good-Enough Citizen: Female Citizenship and Independence," in *Beyond Justice and Equality: Citizenship; Feminist Politics; Female Subjectivity,* eds. Gisela Bock and Susan James (New York: Routledge, 1992).

Josephson, Jyl, *Gender, Families and the State: Child Support Policy in the United States* (Lanham, MD: Rowman and Littlefield, 1997).

Justice: Alternative Political Perspectives, ed. James Sterba (Belmont, CA: Wadsworth, 1980).

Kaufman, Natalie Hevener, and David Whiteman, "Opposition to Human Rights Treaties in the United States Senate: The Legacy of the Bricker Amendment," *Human Rights Quarterly,* vol. 10 (1988).

Keller, Evelyn Fox, *Reflections on Gender and Science* (New Haven, CT: Yale University Press, 1985).

Kirkpatrick, Jeanne, *Dictatorships and Double Standards* (New York: Simon and Schuster, 1982).

Kofman, Eleonore, and Gillian Youngs, eds., *Globalization: Theory and Practice* (New York: Pinter, 1996).

Lacey, Michael J., and Knud Haakonssen, eds., *A Culture of Rights* (Cambridge, MA: Cambridge University Press, 1991).

Langley, Winston E., and Vivian C. Fox, eds., *Women's Rights in the United States: A Documentary History* (Westport, CT: Greenwood Press, 1994).

"Law and the Status of Women," an international symposium, edited by *The Columbia Human Rights Law Review,* vol. 8, no. 1 (1977).

Lillich, Richard B., ed., *U.S. Ratification of Human Rights Treaties: With or Without Reservations?* (Charlottesville: University Press of Virginia, 1981).

Locke, John, *Two Treatises of Government,* ed. Peter Laslett (New York: Cambridge University Press, 1967).

Lynn, Naomi B., ed., *Women, Politics and the Constitution* (New York: Harrington Park Press, 1990).

MacKinnon, Catharine, *Feminism Unmodified: Discourses on Life and Law* (Cambridge, MA: Harvard University Press, 1987).

MacPherson, C. B., *The Life and Times of Liberal Democracy* (New York: Oxford University Press, 1977).

————*The Political Theory of Possessive Individualism: Hobbes to Locke* (New York: Oxford University Press, 1962).

————*The Real World of Democracy* (Oxford, UK: Clarendon, 1966).

Mansbridge, Jane, *Why We Lost the ERA* (Chicago: University of Chicago Press, 1986).

Matas, David, "The Canadian Council for Refugees—Twelve Recommendations on Gender Persecution," *Human Rights Tribune* vol. 1, no. 4 (Winter 1993): 32.

McElroy, Wendy, ed., *Freedom, Feminism and the State* (New York: Holmes and Meier, 1991).

Meehan, Elizabeth, and Selma Sevenhuijsen, eds., *Equality Politics and Gender* (London: Sage, 1991).

Melich, Tanya. *The Republican War against Women: An Insider's Report from behind the Lines* (New York: Bantam, 1996).

Mower, A. Glenn Jr., *The United States, the United Nations, and Human Rights,* no.4 (London: Greenwood, 1979).

Newland, Kathleen, *Women in Politics: A Global Review,* Worldwatch Paper 3 (Washington, DC: Worldwatch Institute, 1975).

Nicholson, Linda J., ed., *Feminism/Postmodernism* (New York and London: Routledge, 1990).

Nussbaum, Martha, and Jonathan Glover, eds., *Women, Culture, and Development: A Study of Human Capabilities* (Oxford: Clarendon Press, 1995.)

Nussbaum, Martha, and Amartya Sen, eds., *The Quality of Life* (Oxford, UK: Clarendon Press, 1993).

Okin, Susan Moller, *Women in Western Political Thought* (Princeton, NJ: Princeton University Press, 1979).

Orentlicher, Diane F., "The United States Commitment to International Human Rights," in *Human Rights and the World Community: Issues and Action,* eds. Richard Pierre Claude and Burns H. Weston (Philadelphia: University of Pennsylvania Press, 1992).

Peterson, V. Spike, ed., *Gendered States: Feminist (Re)Visions of International Relations Theory* (Boulder, CO: Lynne Rienner, 1992).

Phillips, Anne, *Engendering Democracy* (Philadelphia: Pennsylvania State University Press, 1991).

Pickering, Jane M., "Law and the Status of Women in the United States," in *Law and the Status of Women: An International Symposium,* edited by The Columbia Human Rights Law Review (1997).

Pietila, Hilkka and Jeanne Vickers, *Making Women Matter: The Role of the United Nations* (London: Zed,1990).

Przeworski, Adam, *Capitalism and Social Democracy* (New York: Cambridge University Press, 1985).

Rai, Shirin, Hilary Pilkington, and Annie Phizacklea, eds., *Women in the Face of Change: The Soviet Union, Eastern Europe and China* (New York: Routledge, 1992).

Raz, Joseph, *The Morality of Freedom* (Oxford, UK: Clarendon Press, 1986).

Reanda, Laura, "An Approach to Women's Rights," *Human Rights Quarterly,* vol. 3, no.1 (1981).

————"Human Rights and Women's Rights: The United Nations Approach," *Human Rights Quarterly,* vol. 3, no. 2 (1981): 11–31.

Ring, Jennifer, *Modern Political Theory and Contemporary Feminism* (Albany, NY: State University of New York Press, 1991).

Rodley, Nigel, "On the Necessity of United States Ratification of International Human Rights Conventions," in *U.S. Ratification of Human Rights Treaties: With or Without Reservations?* ed. Richard B. Lillich (Charlottesville, VA: University Press of Virginia, 1981).

Romany, Celina, "State Responsibility Goes Private: A Feminist Critique of the Public/Private Distinction in International Human Rights Law," in *Human Rights of Women: National and International Perspectives,* ed. Rebecca J. Cook (Philadelphia: University of Pennsylvania Press, 1994).

Rosenblum, Nancy L., ed., *Liberalism and the Moral Life* (Cambridge, MA: Harvard University Press, 1989).

Rosow, Stephen J., Naeem Inayatullah, and Mark Rupert, eds., *The Global Economy as Political Space* (Boulder, CO: Lynne Rienner, 1994).

Rubenstein, Richard L, *The Cunning of History* (New York: Harper Colophon, 1975).

Rueschemeyer, Marilyn, ed., *Women in the Politics of Postcommunist Eastern Europe* (New York: M. E. Sharpe, 1994).

Russell, Diana E. H., and Nicole Van de Ven, eds., *Crimes Against Women: Proceedings of the International Tribunal* (California: Les Femmes, 1976).

Sainsbury, Diane, ed., *Gendering Welfare States* (London: Sage, 1994).

Sapiro, Virginia, "The Gender Basis of American Social Policy," in *Women, the State and Welfare,* ed. Linda Gordon (Madison: University of Wisconsin Press, 1990).

Shaw, Malcolm N., *International Law* (Cambridge, UK: Grotius, 1991).

Shue, Henry, *Basic Rights: Subsistence, Affluence, and U.S. Foreign Policy* (Princeton, NJ: Princeton University Press, 1980).

Smart, Carol, *Feminism and the Power of Law* (London and New York: Routledge, 1989).

Snow, Clyde Collins, Eric Stover, and Kari Hannibal, "Scientists as Detectives: Investigating Human Rights," *Human Rights and the World Community: Issues and Action,* 2nd. ed., eds., Richard Pierre Claude and Burns H. Weston (Philadelphia: University of Pennsylvania Press, 1992).

Soros, George, *The Crisis of Global Capitalism* (New York: Perseus, 1998).

Stan, Adele M., ed., *Debating Sexual Correctness* (New York: Dell, 1995).

The Stanley Foundation, *Global Changes and Institutional Transformation: Restructuring the Foreign Policymaking Process,* 33rd Strategy for Peace, U.S. Foreign Policy Conference (Muscatine, IA: The Stanley Foundation, 1992).

———,*International Human Rights and US Foreign Policy,* 33rd. Strategy for Peace, U.S. Foreign Policy Conference (Muscatine, IA: The Stanley Foundation, 1992).

———,*The United Nations and Multilateral Sanctions: New Options for US Policy,* 335rd Strategy for Peace, U.S. Foreign Policy Conference (Muscatine, IA: The Stanley Foundation, 1992).

Staudt, Kathleen, ed., *Women, International Development, and Politics* (Philadelphia: Temple University Press, 1990).

Stetson, Dorothy McBride, *Women's Rights in the U.S.A.: Policy Debates and Gender Roles* (Pacific Grove, CA: Brooks/Cole, 1991).

Stiehm, Judith Hicks, ed., *Women's Views of the Political World of Men* (New York: Transnational Publishers, 1984).

Stoltenberg, John, *Refusing to Be a Man: Essays on Sex and Justice* (Portland, OR: Breitenbush, 1989).

Taylor, Charles, *Sources of the Self: The Making of the Modern Identity* (Cambridge, MA: Harvard University Press, 1989).

Thayer, Frederick, *An End to Hierarchy! An End to Competition!: Organizing the Politics and Economics of Survival* (New York: New Viewpoints, 1973).

Tickner, J. Ann, *Gender in International Relations: Feminist Perspectives on Achieving Global Security* (New York: Columbia University Press, 1992).

Tocqueville, Alexis de, *Democracy in America,* ed. Richard D. Heffner (New York: Penguin, 1956).

United Nations Decade for Women, folio (Washington DC: Women's Institute Press, 1987).

United Nations Treaty Series, vol. 1249, no. 20378.

United States Department of State, *Country Reports on Human Rights Practices for 1990,*(Washington, DC: Government Printing Office, 1991).

U.S. Follow-Up to the U.N. Fourth World Conference on Women, The President's Interagency Council on Women (Washington, DC: Government Printing Office, May 1996).

Volkan, Vamik, *The Need to Have Enemies and Allies* (London, UK: Jason Aronson,1994).

Washington NGO Coalition, *Recommendations for Reform in the United Nations Human Rights System,* February 23, 1993.

Weisner, Merry E., *Women and Gender in Early Modern Europe* (Cambridge, UK: Cambridge University Press, 1993).

Weiss, Thomas G., and Leon Gordenker, eds., *NGOs, the UN, and Global Governance* (Boulder, CO: Lynne Rienner, 1996).

West, Robin, *Narrative, Authority, and the Law* (Ann Arbor: University of Michigan Press, 1993).

Weston, Burns, Robin Ann Lukes and Kelly M. Hnatt, "Regional Human Rights Regimes: A Comparison and Appraisal," in *Human Rights and the World Community: Issues and Action,* 2nd. ed., eds. Richard Pierre Claude and Burns H. Weston (Philadelphia: University of Pennsylvania Press, 1992).

Wiseberg, Laurie S., and Harry M. Scoble, "Monitoring Human Rights Violations: The Role of Non-governmental Organizations," in *Human Rights and American Foreign Policy,* eds. Donald Kommers and Gilbert Loescher (Notre Dame, IN: University of Notre Dame Press, 1979).

Woolf, Virginia, *Three Guineas* (San Diego: Harcourt, Brace, 1938).

Women in the Front Line, an Amnesty International Report (Washington, DC: John D. Lucas Printing, Dec. 1990).

Zoelle, Diana G., Lecture by Professor Edy Kaufman, University of Maryland Department of Government and Politics (GOVT 808B): February 4, 1993.

Index